An Integral Ecology
and The Catholic Vision

by
Anthony J Kelly CSsR

An Integral Ecology
and The Catholic Vision

by
Anthony J Kelly CSsR

ATF Theology
Adelaide

2016

Creator: Kelly, Anthony, 1938- author.

Title: Laudato si' : an integral ecology and the Catholic vision / Anthony Kelly.

ISBN: 9781925486193 (paperback)
      9781925486209 (hardback)
      9781925486216 (ebook : epub)
      9781925486223 (ebook : Kindle)
      9781925486230 (ebook : pdf)

Notes: Includes bibliographical references and index.

Subjects: Catholic Church. Pope (2013- : Francis). Laudato si'.
Catholic Church--Doctrines.
Human ecology--Religious aspects.
Environmental responsibility--Religious aspects.
Environmental responsibility--Moral and ethical aspects.
Ecotheology.
Climatic changes--Effect of human beings on.

Dewey Number: 261.88

Cover original artwork:
Photographs
Cover design by Astrid Sengkey
Layout/Artwork by Chris Powell

Text Minion Pro Size 11 & 12

Published by:

An imprint of the ATF Press Publishing
Group owned by ATF (Australia) Ltd.
PO Box 504
Hindmarsh, SA 5007
ABN 90 116 359 963

Dedicated

to my colleagues in the Faculty of Theology and Philosophy

at Australian Catholic University

CONTENTS

INTRODUCTION

On Pentecost Sunday, May 24, 2015, Pope Francis issued his encyclical letter on ecology and climate, entitled *Laudato Si: On Care for our Common Home.*[1] The encyclical itself is quite a 'game-changer', in terms of Catholic teaching and its dialogue with science, and in the field of ecumenical and even interreligious collaboration and communication. What follows is a theological response to the document, not in any negative sense, but as teasing out the implications of fundamental doctrinal and spiritual topics, most of which explicitly figure in the encyclical, but, because of its length, cannot be given much space. Needless to say, these theological elaborations are my own, even though I have aligned them with passages in the encyclical where these topics are treated or alluded to.

The phrase, 'integral ecology' appears quite often in the encyclical. It suggests the many aspects of what is involved in addressing environmental questions dealing with 'care for our common home'. This entails a widespread collaborative effort, not only on the part of the sciences and economics, but including all the human concerns that are the domain of anthropology, sociology, politics, and art, and much more—since no one can be left out of the conversation. As already mentioned, my contribution to this 'integral ecology' is more in the areas covered by theology, philosophy and spirituality— which means practising a proper docility as regards the scientific analyses of the situation, and leaving to experts such questions of climate change, desertification, ocean warming and the like. I hope,

---

1. Pope Francis, *Laudato Si: On Care for our Common Home* (Vatican City: Editrice Vaticana, 2015). Note that numbers in square brackets refer to numbered paragraphs of the encyclical.

1

however, that this collaborative division of considerations will not cause theological topics such as creation, incarnation, Trinity and so forth to sound too ethereal, let alone irrelevant, given the ever-expanding dialogue that must take place. In a world of dwindling resources, it is as well to stress the necessity of the ever-renewable resources of Christian faith and hope. Ecological concerns can occasion serious levels of depression and disillusionment, unless such ecology is truly 'integral' in allowing for the spiritual resources that can come from religious faith. Faith may not provide a detailed program, let alone new information, but it does inspire hope and a sense of living in in environment in which the Word became flesh, and in a universe called into existence by God's creative love. It is also my hope that, by evoking this larger religious horizon, the danger of ideological divisiveness and monodimensional mindsets might be avoided. Ecology is a serious business, and those involved either theoretically or practically, know the stress of contradication and opposition. A genuinely integral ecology works in the largest possible horizon while being informed at every step by the contributions of those who have a paricular expertise. There will be inevitably opposing points of views even though there are new modes of collaboration to be discovered, and more inclusive and respectful conversations to be conducted. It seems that the development of an integral ecology is at an early stage, and for tht reason I humbly offer this theological contribution.

This plan of this book is simple: a chapter 1 (Perspectives) focussing on various approaches to the encyclical itself, is followed by a further six chapters on what Pope Francis mentions but does not develop, for example, Creation, Incarnation, Trinity, Eucharist, Death and Christian Conversion—all are ingredients in an 'integral ecology'. I take up these topics in my own way and range of reference, and include at least one topic that the encyclical barely mentions, namely, death, for it is a rather obvious biological, ecological and human fact!

I now offer a brief note on each of these chapters in the order in which they appear. Chapter 1, 'The Encyclical: Seven Perspectives', stresses the point, in the words of the Pope, that 'unless we struggle with the deeper issues, I do not believe that our concern for ecology will produce significant results' [160]. Ecological conversion is envisaged as a long path of renewal and progress on many levels [197], in the recognition of our common earthly origins,[2] and our participation in this community of living things needs to find hope for a shared future. There are some seven perspectives to be kept in mind, each of which throws light on the interconnection of integral ecology and the Incarnation:

1. The special *Inspiration* deriving from St Francis of Assisi. In him the love of God, the neighbour and the neighbourhood were uniquely represented so as to remain an abiding inspiration.

2. *Ecology and Consumerism* notes that ecological integrity is compromised when market forces so colonise the imagination as to turn the human being first of all into a consumer—to the neglect of a larger world and a larger humanity. The Pope quotes the *Earth Charter* of 2000: 'Let ours be a time remembered for the awakening of a new reverence for life, the firm resolve to achieve sustainability, the quickening of the struggle for justice and peace, and the joyful celebration of life.'

3. *Problems to be faced* are many when society is caught up in a whirlwind of consumerism. The most educated do not possess the authority or skill or wisdom capable of offering guidance on a global scale. Modern life is felt to be a 'seedbed for collective selfishness' [204]. The well-being of whole countries can be sacrificed to economic imperatives of efficiency and profit.

---

2. See Brendan Purcell, *From Big Bang to Big Mystery: Human Origins in the Light of Creation and Evolution* (New York:New City Press,2013).

4. More positively, *Dialogue and Collaboration.* In a critical situation, new beginnings presuppose a capacity for buoyant dialogue, lest the way forward collapse into ideological conflicts and violent confrontations [163]. The aim is to generate processes capable of incorporating a great variety of viewpoints [178], and with a long term outcome in mind.

5. *The Church and Ecology.* Vatican II's 'the Church in the Modern World' becomes, not only the Church in the *postmodern* world characterised by and endless play of relative viewpoints, but now the Church in the *ecological* world at a particularly crucial time, earthed in the ecological integrity of this planet. There is need, then, for the Church to be the agent and even the embodiment to an 'integral ecology'.

6. *The Gift* counters the stifling self-absorption of modern anthropocentrism which has dulled the capacity to receive life and existence as a gift, even to the point of demeaning the role of the human in the world of creation [115]. There are, however, real limits to human activity if stewardship is to be responsible. The intimate interconnections of all beings in the mystery of life on this planet must be acknowledged [117–118].

7. *Human Nature in the Natural World* asks how our evolutionary emergence affects a notion of integral ecology? We cannot neglect the generic 'animality' of the human condition. By recovering the 'animal' within us, we more adequately understand ourselves.

The risen and ascended Christ is not contained by creation, but he himself already contains and fills the universe [83]: all things are made through him and for him and in him. Through the incarnation of the Word [99], God has claimed the world as his own. God is present from the beginning, and is ever-present in a hidden manner within the natural world. [100, 221].

Chapter 2, 'Creator, Creation and ecology': the 'deeper issue' here concerns the meaning of life, existence and our work in the world. Of radical relevance are the mystery of creation and the character of the Creator, for these affect our sense of reality—human, environmental and cosmic. Discussion of such topics can enrich integral ecology, and point more deeply into that ever-renewable resource from which Christian faith can draw.

Chapter 3, 'The Incarnation and Integral Ecology' considers the incarnation as a focal doctrine of faith. But its reality is not only a truth, for it inspires feelings and shapes sensibilities as it informs Christian consciousness, underpins relationships and inspires action. It is, therefore, constitutive of human identity and subjectivity. The Word made flesh affects the sense of self and the depth and range of its participation in the world as 'our common home'.

Chapter 4, 'Trinitarian Connection'. Urgent, earthly concerns, do not readily recognize the relevance of the doctrine of the Trinity. Nonetheless, an integral ecology can make a fertile connections between 'care for our earthly home' and the trinitarian life of God. The goal is to suggest the trinitarian dimension of all creation and the manner in which it is connected within the one divine creative mystery. This can lead to a profound appreciation of our common terrestrial home, and the communion of life and existence it represents.

Chapter 5, 'A Eucharistic Ecology'. The Eucharist inspires a genuinely integral ecology. It brings nature and culture together precisely by relating them to the Body of Christ. The 'real presence' of the whole Christ is communicated to the community through the transformation of the shared 'fruit of the earth and the work of human hands'. Through the power of the Spirit, the bread becomes our 'bread of life', just as the wine that is offered becomes 'our spiritual drink'. Thus, the earthy elements that sustain human life and communication have an essential place in the 'ecology' of God's self-giving in Christ.

Chapter 6, 'Integral Ecology and Sister Death', Clearly, Pope Francis has no romantic view of nature, given his robust denunciation of consumerism, his sensitivity to the sufferings of the earth and its people, his lamentation over the disappearance of so many species of fauna and flora, and his special reference to the deaths of the poor and infants [20, 20, 48].[3] All these are evidences of a sober realism. Nonetheless, there is little mention of death in *Laudato Si'*. Nor does it include in the citation of the Canticle of St Francis the verse the saint added as his own death approached, 'Be praised my Lord through our Sister Bodily Death, ,From whose embrace no living person can escape'. In the interests of a genuine integral ecology, therefore, this chapter considers the ecological and theological significance of death and how it affects and inspires 'care for our common home'.

Chapter 7, 'Ecological Conversion' that has become necessary in these times of environmental crisis relies on the hope that, with the grace of God, a radical change of mind and heart is possible. It is, of course, a religious event, but it contains and inspires a change on the level of morality and in the intellectual horizon. Ecological conversion also affects the sense of self in a psychological way and makes one see the world in a hopeful manner. It finds expression in hopeful vocations—classically speaking, in religious life, and today increasingly in married and family life, in changes in life-style, in care for the environment and for all who are oppressed and disadvantaged.

These seven chapters find their focus in the incarnation of the Word just as their purpose is to extend the field in which an integral ecology can work. I have presented them in a particular sequence, but I realise other ways of ordering this material would make good sense. Indeed, it is possible to begin at the end and consider this whole exploration as a way of extending what ecological conversion

---

3.   All references to the text of the Encyclical will follow the paragraph numbers Pope Francis' Encyclical Letter, *Laudato Si'*, *On Care for Our Common Home* (Vatican City: Editrice Vaticana, 2015). Numbers in square brackets correspond to the numbered paragraphs in *Laudato Si'*.

might mean. Some might prefer to start with focal topic of the Incarnation and go on to consider how it is 'earthed' in the ecology of this planet. There are many possible choices, but the main thing is to keep on exploring the Incarnation as an ever expanding feature of God's activity, and reflect on how an integral ecology might itself expand in the light of Christian faith in creation, Incarnation, Trinity, Eucharist—and the mystery of death itself. That faith has entered into an exciting new phase by being more grounded and 'earthed' in the fate of this planet. The Church as the communion of those who share this faith is finding its own community and mission realigned by awakening to what promises to be a far-reaching ecological conversion. Finally, ecology itself can discover new dimensions of the communion of life by working with the great virtues of faith, hope, and charity, along true humility, to bring about an authentic integrity as an open-ended dialogue and generous collaboration with all forms of science, scholarship and art.

Anthony Kelly CSsR
Feast of All Saints, 2015.

1

The Encyclical[1]: Seven Perspectives

The following pages are a response to questions Pope Francis has raised concerning 'the deeper issues' involved in a seriously Christian ecological conversion and care for the environment of planet Earth: 'unless we struggle with the deeper issues, I do not believe that our concern for ecology will produce significant results' [160]. At best we will be dealing with symptoms, not treating the disease. What is at stake is our sense of the human vocation and the whole meaning of life out of which to enjoy the blessings of life in 'our common home', and face up to the problems we have caused.

Ecological conversion is envisaged as a long path of renewal and progress on many levels, in politics, collaboration and imagination [197]. That journey forward must be energised by an awareness of our common earthly origins,[2] alert to the ways we, and the whole community of living things, belong together in hope for a shared future:

> It cannot be emphasized enough how everything is interconnected. Time and space are not independent of one another, and not even atoms or subatomic particles can be considered in isolation. Just as the different aspects of the planet—physical, chemical and biological—are interrelated, so, too, living species are part of a network which we will never fully explore and understand [138].

---

1. Note that numbers in square brackets correspond to the paragraphs in *Laudato Si'*.
2. See Brendan Purcell, *From Big Bang to Big Mystery: Human Origins in the Light of Creation and Evolution* (New York: New City Press, 2013).

The environmental network is a complex system of relationships in which the higher are pre-formed in the lower. What is presumed is the successive emergence of atoms, neurones and DNA molecules, cells, organs, organisms, bodies, bondings, populations, and the eco-systems serving life on this planet; and ultimately speaking, participation in the divine life itself. In short, 'Everything is interconnected . . . genuine care for our own lives and our relationships with nature is inseparable from fraternity, justice and faithfulness to others' [70]. The breadth of the horizon in which the encyclical is expressed reaches even to the very life of God: 'Everything is interconnected, and this invites us to develop a spirituality of that global solidarity which flows from the mystery of the Trinity' [240].

The encyclical deals with six major areas. Chapter 1 reflects on what is happening to the earth as our common home. Chapter 2, 'Creator, Creation and Ecology', points to the horizon against which problems can be faced and answers sought. Chapter 3 moves to the human roots of the ecological crisis. Chapter 4 shows a way forward through an 'integral ecology'. Chapter 5 moves to what is entailed in this integral ecology, with its lines of approach and modes of action. The final chapter 6 indicates what is required for a continuing process of renewal. The 'lengthy and troubling' reflection [246], with its two hundred and forty-six paragraphs ends, as it began, with prayer—a prayer for the earth, and a prayer in union with all creation.

The scope of the document and the questions it raises is so huge that it resists any easy summary. The remarks that follow in this first chapter of our response are of a more general and perspectival character, even though precise references [in square brackets] to the particular paragraphs in the document are offered. We will be concentrating more particularly on chapters 2 and 4 of the encyclical. The aim is to suggest a sense of the ever-renewable resources to be found in faith and spirituality for a world suffering an environmental crisis. Non-renewable traditional sources of material energy such as fossil-fuels are being urgently re-assessed. It might be, also, that the culture as a whole is lacking the vision and the energy to diagnose and respond to the plight of our common home. Hence, this perspectival treatment will lead into particular spiritual and theological issues referred to, touched on, or presumed, in the encyclical, such as creation, incarnation, Trinity, Eucharist, death and eschatological hope in the chapters to follow. We hope, therefore, to clarify and extend the horizon in which an integral ecology[3] can continue to develop. This is a modest contribution, given the urgency of so many scientific, economic, social, political, cultural and anthropological issues demanding the attention of this and future generations. Yet there is one, ever-renewable and inexhaustible resource. Without it, the grace and mercy that sustain hope, miseries can only increase.

1. The Inspiration

In his treatment of 'care for our common home', Pope Francis enlarges on his Franciscan inspiration. He expresses in the words of the great saint of Assisi, the praise of God echoing through all creation; and, in consequence, the loving solidarity of all in this one creation. All creatures come from God, reveal the beauty of God, and are moving toward God for their fulfilment. St Francis is fittingly the patron of ecology, for, through his witness, the love of God, love for all creation and love for the poorest came to striking expression [66, 87].

Different saints exert their respective influences in a variety of historical situations. St Athanasius emerged as the champion of orthodoxy in the struggle against early heresies. St Benedict laid the foundations of a new Europe with his monastic foundations. The intellectual influence of St Thomas Aquinas has proved remarkably durable since the time of the founding of the great medieval universities and centres of learning. Catherine of Siena brought a grace of unity and reconciliation to a deeply divided church. Teresa

---

3.   The phrase first appears in a 2009 document of the International Theological Commission which recognises the need for the Catholic 'natural law' tradition to be open to ecological perspectives—and for these to recognise a fundamental natural law. See, 'In search of universal ethic: A New Look at Natural Law', paragraph 82.

and John of the Cross witnessed to the deeper reaches of Christian experience at a time when the need was to go beyond doctrinal formulations and divisions, to the fundamental issue of union with God. St Ignatius brought a fresh missionary and educational impulse to Catholic life. St Alphonsus Liguori brought the blessing of moral balance to Christian conscience torn between the extremes of rigorism and laxity. Blessed John Henry Newman helped in the understanding the development of doctrines leading up to the time of Vatican II. St Therese of Lisieux recalled Christian piety to the simplicity of love and self-surrender at the dawn of the twentieth century. Clearly, Pope Francis is promoting St Francis of Assisi as the special patron of the Church at this time of a demanding ecological conversion. The future will be a time of hope, sometimes painful conflict and even suffering. Francis' love for God and all creation, together his conformity to the crucified Christ, make him an inspiring presence in the communion of saints.

Following this inspiration, *Laudato Si'* is a bracing reflection on the connections between the love of God and neighbour, in ways that necessarily include the 'neighbourhood' of planet earth itself, and the global commons of the air, water and soils of this biosphere. We might also add to the worldwide web as a new 'global commons' of interconnectivity and communication, a powerful means of bringing to consciousness our common membership of life on planet Earth. In other words, earthed in this one planetary environment, we come to God and relate to one another as *earthlings*, participating in a unique, many-splendored, delicate and increasingly vulnerable biosphere—the matrix of the co-existence of all living things on planet Earth. To forget that is to fail in true humility. As the liturgy of Ash Wednesday reminds all who are signed with the blessed ashes, we 'are but dust and unto dust we shall return'. We are born of this earth and live together on this planet, the nurturing environment and milieu of our existence [1–2; 10].

The worn-out metaphor of the 'global village' suggests that a small minority of the world's people live in splendid isolation within gated communities, but consume most of the produce, own most of the natural resources, and control the means of production. In its best connotation, however, globalisation connotes a newly emerging stage in world history. Despite the differences and divisions inherited from the past—in relation to different geographical locations, nations, languages, cultures and religions—a new consciousness is emerging. In the background there is a growing awareness of the larger cosmic story of planet Earth, and the emergence of our humanity out of a long evolutionary history spanning the immensity of space and time. Humanity can now situate itself within a 14.7 billion year pre-history.[4] As a result, human consciousness awakens to a new humility. To be aware of the uncanny emergence of the cosmos, and of the singularity of life on this planet, is to live with a new sense of proportion. Whatever our national, ethnic, cultural or religious differences, we have a common origin within an unimaginably immense and fecund cosmic process. Given the sheer contingency of our existence, despite the infinitesimal insignificance of our physical being in the physical universe, human consciousness has a unique capacity to ask big questions: what is the significance of human existence? How do we belong together? How should we collaborate to bring a distinctively human contribution to the history of life in which we participate? Cosmic humility undermines all egocentric pretensions. The universal order into which all are born does not revolve around any particular individual, group, nation or culture. A self-centred pride appears as the ultimate absurdity, and the destructive conflicts to which it gives rise are a profound dislocation of the reality in which we share.

2. Ecology and Consumerism

Pope Francis calls on both Church and world to what he terms, 'an integral ecology'. From a scientific point of view, most of us will have to take on faith the findings of science on climate change, desertification, and other local and global threats to the

---

4.   Celia Deane-Drummond, *The Wisdom of the Liminal; Evolution and Other Animals in Human Becoming* (Grand Rapids, Michigan: Eerdmans, 2014).

environment. On the other hand, we all intimately know about the power of consumerism and its pervasive influence. Its aim is to make us imagine ourselves in terms of a consumer world. That means adopting a consumer identity, with the result that an extraordinary dislocation occurs. An artificial image begins to precede the reality. We become increasingly what the all-powerful market needs us to be. Even our politicians are turned into carefully crafted media images. The reality of who they are or what they stand for is of little importance. Public figures in art, sport, science, and the media are co-opted by financial enticements to lend their weight to the general illusion. Great classical music, biblical and literary images, works of art, historical events and personages, are all plundered as raw material for the consumerist message: 'I consume, therefore I am'. Some have a first-hand experience of harm suffered by the environment through mining, rising sea levels, bad urban planning, polluted waterways, soil erosion and exhaustion. All this presumes a crisis in non-renewable resources. On the other hand, there are the ever-renewable resources of hope and faith by which the future can be faced in the confidence that the Creator of all is summoning us to a new era of respect for creation in all its forms.

It goes without saying, that human beings are not only consumers or destroyers of the environment. Nothing can completely suppress in the human spirit the attraction of the good, the true and the beautiful [205]. Moreover, there is no limit to the incalculable workings of grace in our hearts. If the possibilities of change are not recognised, human dignity is compromised. Ecological conversion, whether it occurs from above by the grace of God or grows from below by renewed efforts to explore and act, is the basis for a new lifestyle capable of carrying its convictions into the political, economic and social world. In surrender to God, we can transcend ourselves in concern for others [204, 208], and so move beyond self-centeredness. That will be necessary if we are to genuinely care for our neighbour and the natural environment. The Pope echoes the Earth Charter issued at the beginning of this century:

As never before in history, common destiny beckons us to seek a new beginning . . . Let ours be a time remembered for the awakening of a new reverence for life, the firm resolve to achieve sustainability, the quickening of the struggle for justice and peace, and the joyful celebration of life [*Earth Charter*, The Hague (29 June 2000).]

3. Problems Resulting

Prospects can be grim for an ecologically attuned conscience [203]. The driven, chaotic life of the modern city often offends human dignity [154]. To the degree we are caught up in a whirlwind of needless buying and selling, the economy tends to promote extreme consumerism in everyone. Even those most educated in our societies do not possess the authority or skill or wisdom capable of offering guidance on a global scale when modern life is felt to be a 'seedbed for collective selfishness' [204]. The global reach of economic power, with its enormous capabilities of instant communication unhampered by geographical and national barriers, its huge fund of available capital, is biased against more humane considerations of a sustainable environment. The well-being of whole countries can be sacrificed to economic imperatives of efficiency and profit. The imbalance of this situation calls for a revaluation of the economic arrangements so that commercial enterprises cease being a law unto themselves. How a new economic order might respect a larger scale of values, especially when the widespread consumerist delirium is so wasteful in regard to the environment, is no small challenge.

In the meantime, a great emptiness threatens; a void in the heart filled only by the compulsion to buy, own, and consume [161]. Living beyond our means has exhausted the planet and led to catastrophic outcomes. A self-centred culture of instant gratification is ineffective when it comes to addressing present problems and for preparing for the future. Any sense of the common good, for present or future generations, shrinks to a vague aspiration, especially when national interest predominates over international responsibility.

Thus, the integrity expected of individual conscience is not readily presumed on national level. No one with any sense of human history or society can doubt that legitimate areas of national autonomy and self-determination must be respected.[5] But a self-regarding national autonomy does not easily cohere with global ecological responsibility. The principle of national self-determination need not mean that national or cultural forms of egoism must prevail over concern for the global environment.

Clearly, the problem is many-sided. The Pope with careful understatement remarks that 'each age tends to have only a meagre sense of its own limitations' [105]. Only with difficulty, and something of a conversion, can any era see or feel anything beyond its present horizons and concerns. In this respect, our times suffer the limits of an entrenched technocratic and economic paradigm, even to the point of dominating national sports, and shaping them to serve commercial interests. A forward-looking vision is especially blinkered by a mono-dimensional idea of progress. It regards environmental issues as merely secondary to the real issues of productivity, economic value, and efficiency. The limits of such an outlook point to the need for the integral ecology already mentioned. In the first place, a holistic vision will presume an appreciation of the planetary biosphere, and show the capacity to diagnose how it has been harmed by uncaring exploitation. But it is not enough if such outer, objective ecology is unrelated to the 'inner ecology' of culture. Without a conversion of mind and heart, in a both a personal and social sense, there can be little hope for any turn-around in our relationship to world of nature and the delicate interrelationships and synergies it discloses. Further, without a shareable discourse on basic human values, the prospects of considering the common good or the integrity of the environment diminish. Efforts to transcend individual and sectional interests would result in endless litigation— thus serving the manipulations of the most powerful. As an element in an integral ecology, the traditional notion of 'natural law' has

---

5.   See Elias Baumgarten, 'In Search of a Morally Acceptable Nationalism', in *Journal of Ecumenical Studies* 42/3 (Summer 2007): 355–362.

a perennial appeal in a way that was not specific to any religion, philosophy, national and political interests. But problems remain . . .

The more an economic paradigm is globally imposed, the more limited and one-dimensional the idea of progress becomes. It can fail to notice an increasingly depleted earth, and, for that matter, an increasingly oppressed and depressed humanity [107]. In this respect, the global economic paradigm is like a huge locomotive. A fast train might seem as a desirable option for covering huge distances in a safe and convenient manner. But once the tracks are laid, the direction is fixed, no detours are possible. What is more, travelling in a fast train is not the best way to explore the natural environment. The train must keep moving on, unaware of the flowers, trees, lakes and rivers, the valleys and hills, the birds and animals, and the people of the countryside. Of course, speed of transport can be necessary for other reasons; but the more pragmatic the trip, the more there is danger of 'tedious monotony and a sense of emptiness' [113–114], as travellers are locked into their own limited purposes and block out everything else. This image of railway conveniently illustrates how technology shapes our experience. Indeed, it may inspire 'unrestrained delusions of grandeur' [114] beyond any realistic sense of proportion. Everything is reduced to getting there—arriving at a destination, enclosed inside an air-conditioned carriage of steel and glass, without a concern for anything but present comfort and the intended destination [91]. In such a case, a particular technology completely shapes the outlook of the travellers so as to render them unaware the cost of the journey in terms of environmental degradation, and any larger sense of direction and social belonging.

Given the force and pervasiveness of the technocratic model of progress, any other cultural paradigm is all-but inconceivable. If you are travelling by rail you are not going by boat or flying by plane, and certainly not making a pilgrimage on foot. Yet some vast change in mind and heart must occur if this planet is to be our human homeland in the future. Admittedly, there is a certain terror associated with facing the situation as it is. For the present state of affairs is clouded by the commercial media which, to a large degree, is a vast consumer-driven machine, not only in pushing products, but even producing the kind of news judged to be of general interest—usually, the bad news of scandal, violence and celebrity antics.

The inner environment of whole societies is distorted when it is deliberately colonised by images and associations designed to direct the choices of consumers. As mentioned above, even the patrimony of culture has been mined to this purpose as when a particular product is presented with a few bars of Mozart, and the natural images of sea, and light and region, and family life are linked to consumer products—cars, domestic appliances, medications, cosmetics and machines. The overall aim, however implicit, is to reduce the quality of life to economic terms, to what can be owned, used for one's own enjoyment and directed to one's own security.

On the other hand, there is no room for moralistic depression. Not only must our reaction be brought into contact with the ever-renewable resource of trust in God and faith in Christ, it must make use of the best intellectual resources. Problems can be solved by human ingenuity, especially when directed to environmental ends and informed by the wisdom of an integral ecology. Still, there seems to be a strange ecological forgetfulness in the mindset of technocracy. The dominant paradigm has long been fixated on power, control, and exploitation with little care for the integrity of the environment [102]. The problem consists not only in the runaway character of the economic imperative, but also in a shrinking outlook:

> The specialization which belongs to technology makes it difficult to see the larger picture. The fragmentation of knowledge proves helpful for concrete applications, and yet it often leads to a loss of appreciation for the whole, for the relationships between things, and for the broader horizon [91].

When each area of knowledge or expertise exists in its own defensive silo, dialogue and collaboration are realised with great difficulty. The 'complex problems of today's world, particularly those regarding the environment and the poor . . . cannot be dealt with from a single perspective or from a single set of interests' [91]. Each area of knowledge must enter a larger framework of collaboration with other fields of expertise, such as philosophy and social ethics. That cannot happen suddenly. Specialists are trained to master only a particular area, as a result ethical considerations or the desirability of a larger dialogue and collaboration cannot but appear as distracting from the particular area of one's specialisation [91]. Consequently, every area of human intelligence must not only have a heart in addressing the sufferings of humanity and of the planet itself, but also become more fully and deeply intelligent. On that point, Pope Francis observes that the lessons of the Global Financial Crisis of 2007–8 have yet to be absorbed [109]. Despite the enormity of problems in the present, the hope expressed in *Laudato Si'* is for the long-term. It looks to a change of heart and mind, in organisation, communication and education, and in all institutions necessary for the development of an ecological culture [111]. There is no question of being anti-science, since science in all its forms belongs in an integral ecology [182]. On the other hand, environmental impact assessments must come before business proposals based on individual, group or even national profit.

4. Dialogue and Collaboration

In a critical situation, any new beginning presupposes a capacity for buoyant dialogue, lest the way forward collapse into ideological conflicts and violent confrontations [163]. Dialogue can be simply a catchword for any attempt to be polite. What is at stake, however, is neither mere civility nor scoring points in a debate, nor simply the determination to keep talking in the face of contradiction. The aim is to generate processes capable of incorporating a great variety of viewpoints [178], and with a long term outcome in mind. If frank dialogue in the service of life conducted in a spirit of ecological concern and transparency [186, 189] is the goal, it also recognises that 'market forces alone are not a magic answer.

There is the question of an 'integral ecology' as already mentioned. The word, 'ecology', was coined little more than a century ago by the German zoologist, Ernst Häckel. Its Greek roots imply, 'the meaning of the home', and it came to refer to the study of the complex totality of conditions necessary for the survival of living organisms in a particular environment. These varied forms of life are symbiotically interrelated within the one matrix or web of life on planet Earth. Thus, ecology explores nature 'in the round', so to speak, alert to all the intricate, delicate interactions that characterise life on this planet. Planetary life emerges as a biological community of communities in which each living thing and each species is not an isolated self-contained entity, but participates in a living, interconnected totality.

The biophysical character of ecological interdependence in nature suggests further extensions of the meaning of ecology to the interdependence and mutual conditioning of different realities in the realm of society, culture and human consciousness, hence an *integral* ecology Human beings do not live by instinct in a particular habitat, but inhabit the open world of meaning and moral responsibility. In contrast to other animals, the human species is necessarily a participant in the intellectual and moral formation of a global environment. From one point of view, our humanity is a given, a *datum*—what each of us is born with; from another, it is a program—what we make of ourselves and our world, and the ways we can 'mean the world' to one another with intelligence and responsibility.

An *integral* ecology, if it is to provide a comprehensive sense of the whole, must allow not only for the data of the senses regarding what can be measured, weighed and calculated [199], but also explore the meaning and values accessible through human intelligence, imagination, artistic creativity, the wisdom of faith, moral experience and the compassion that only love can give. Science needs to be methodologically open to the whole of reality, just as believers, through their orientation to love, justice and peace, can bring a new appreciation to the findings of science, and provide new energies in the implementation of good government policy. Integral ecology, inspired by hope as it is, offers a radical vision able to counteract the so-called 'silo mentality' of disciplinary specialisations, for these tend to be each locked into its own limited sphere of competence. Likewise, an integral ecology presupposes a dialogue among ecological movements as the only way to get beyond rigid ideologies. Moreover, essential to integral ecology is continuing interreligious dialogue intent on recognising and responding to the sufferings of the world's peoples in a context of compassion [201], and in order to create an environment of hope and gratitude. Religions, in their various traditions, contribute to the common good [156–8] and the recognition of human dignity, especially that of the most defenceless who have suffered most from environmental destruction.

5. The Church and Ecology

With this encyclical, Vatican II's 'the Church in the Modern World' becomes, not only the Church in the *postmodern* world characterised by an endless play of relative viewpoints, but now the Church in the *ecological* world at a particularly crucial time, earthed in the ecological integrity of this planet. Whether it be traditional natural law thought or the integral ecology of Pope Francis, the Apostle Paul gives a lead when he encourages the Christian community of Philippi: 'Whatever is true, whatever is honourable, whatever is just, whatever is pure, whatever is pleasing, whatever is commendable, if there is any excellence and if there is anything worthy of praise, think about these things' (Phil 4:8). That 'whatever' is the beginning of the Church's contribution to an integral ecology, at this present time. Similarly, the oft-cited declaration of *Gaudium et Spes* takes on a new intensity and scope:

> The joy and hope, the grief and anguish of the people of our time, especially of those who are poor and afflicted in any way, are the joy and hope, the grief and anguish of the followers of Christ as well (GS#1).

Pope Francis, exercising his ecclesiastical and moral authority for the Church and the world as a whole, is addressing all people on the theme of their common home. The mission of the Church to the world necessarily opens to the mission of the Church within the world the biosphere of this planet. The traditional mission of the Church to all nations finds concrete expression in what concerns all peoples, namely the earth itself, especially as it is now increasingly undergoing the environmental crisis brought about by human self-destructiveness. There is need, then, for the Church to be the agent and even the embodiment of an "integral ecology", open to every aspect of the problem and its possible solution. Though there remain many different points of view in diagnosing and addressing the environmental problems of the present, the Church can ensure that a new dialogue take place—open to everyone [14], in a new spirit of solidarity with all who care for our earthly home, and in cooperation with God, the source of life and our ultimate destiny. Such a widespread dialogue will not necessarily be a gently conducted conversation, but one open to 'forthright and honest debate' on any number of contentious issues. The Church is institutionally well positioned when it comes to establishing priories for the future, in education and pastoral empowerment [14–15). The vitality of the Church is shown in its ability to re-found or reconstitute itself in every age of its history, in response to signs of the times in the sufferings and needs of the present. For the Church at this moment, the cry of the earth and cry of the poor cannot be separated. In other words, the ecological well-being of the planet and the social well-being of the oppressed and under-privileged, are interrelated [49–50].

By implication, peace, justice and the preservation of the environment are three interconnected thematic concerns [92]. No one of these can exist without the others. If any one of them is omitted, the others are reduced. An overall vision finds its focus in the one love of God uniting humanity and the world in a common pilgrimage to the fullness of life. That movement presumes that the poor and the most powerless possess natural rights [94], and cannot be regarded as casualties to progress, nor as raw material to be exploited. In an environmental horizon, a social perspective is therefore essential. The earth and the whole natural environment are gifts destined for all to share. As the giver, the source of this collective good, the God of love has no favourites. No person or people or country may possess God-given exclusive rights over any part of the environment [93]. Though private property is generally a condition for human flourishing, there is a social mortgage on what we own and on the level of our consumption of resources [95]. The fundamental consideration is the common good of all, in the present, and for the future [159].

What then is the significance of the Church in this global ecological conversion? In prayer and repentance, in its trinitarian character, Eucharistic celebrations and eschatological hope, the Church can witness to the meaning of 'integral ecology'. The wisdom of faith points in the direction of new collaboration between faith, scientific reason, social action, art and philosophy—all intent on environmental integrity [113]. These aspects of conversion are to be understood as dynamically interacting and developing so that the best intelligence, the best practice, and the best collaboration are informed by the God-given and God-directed energies of faith, hope and charity. To heal the planetary environment requires an ecological conversion of global proportions [4–5]. However, such a wholesale change of heart would be unstable and superficial unless it included an appreciation of the ecology of human existence in all its relationships, along with the meanings and values that shape and direct human development. In this respect, our humanity will be crippled and distorted if it sees itself as detached from the larger environment on which it depends and in which it has a unique role. The living environment is first of all a gift to be received and defended from all forms of debasement and exploitation. Because to be human is itself a gift, because it entails unique responsibilities in relationship to God, to others, and to the planetary environment, it must allow for a radical criticism of the power-structures shaping today's society, culture and its consumerist lifestyle [4–5]. However much the human world has developed and been transformed in the course of history, its gift-like character can never be suppressed. It is not simply a resource to be exploited in an ecologically unconscious and irresponsible economy. Awareness of the God-given gift of life and existence shapes the horizon in which the mission of the Church is conducted, and in which an integral ecology can develop.

This encyclical is not an episodic intervention on a hitherto unnoticed theme. In citing not only the teaching of previous popes, but also many episcopal conferences, it presumes and confirms the concerns of the Catholic Church in many parts of the world.[6] It cites the Ecumenical Patriarch Bartholomew [8, n. 15], and even dips into a collection on Sufi mystics to quote the mystic, Ali Al-Khawas, on the need to find God in the whole of nature [234, n. 159]. Ecumenical developments among the Christian communities in recent decades have not moved toward unity simply by discussing the core doctrines of Christian tradition. There has also been an outward turn, arising from the realisation that all human beings are the beneficiaries of God's saving love and are called to participate in planetary biosphere in a spirit of thanksgiving and justice.[7] The awareness of being part of one web of planetary life, provoked in some measure by writings such as Lynn White's 'The Historical

---

6. For example, the episcopal conferences of South Africa, Latin America and the Caribbean, the Philippines, Bolivia, Germany, The United States, New Zealand, Australia, Canada, Japan, Brazil, Dominican Republic, Paraguay, the Federation of Asian Bishops Conferences, Argentina, Portugal, and Mexico.

7. For example, Pope John Paul II, 'Peace with God the Creator, Peace with all of Creation', World Day for Peace message, 1990; Pope John Paul II and Patriarch Bartholomew I of Constantinople, 'We are Still Betraying the Mandate God Has Given Us': *A Declaration on the Environment*, June 10, 2002; US Catholic Bishops. 'Global Climate Change: A please for Dialogue, Prudence and the Common Good', 2001; ' Christian Faith Statement on Ecology', from the Ecumenical Patriarchate of Constantinople, the World Council of Churches, and the Vatican Franciscan Center of Environmental Studies; 'A Common Declaration on the Environment', by the International Catholic-Jewish Liaison Committee, March 1998. These and many more statements can be accessed through the following links: http://www3.villanova.edu/mission/CSTresource/ecology/front.htm; http://www.shc.edu/theolibrary.environ.htm

Roots of our Ecological Crisis', [8] has both ecumenical and ecological consequences as faith awakens to the whole mystery of life and Christian responsibilities within it. Pope Francis and some eminent theological authors speak of an 'ecological conversion' taking place as an essential dimension of Christian conversion at this time,[9] at least in regard to the development of an environmental conscience and a more general consciousness of the Christian vocation within a planetary biosphere.[10]

The simple metaphor of the spectrum of light points to how Christian communities have begun to be aware of all the colours of the spectrum of faith and human experience, above all, there is the often unnoticed band of green. In the pursuit of Christian unity, the old simplicities of black and white are no longer useful as Christian consciousness grows and expands, unfolding in an astonishingly vast, subtle and beautifully differentiated universe of many colours. Thus faith stretches upward and outward, to the One who dwells in 'unapproachable light' (1 Tim 6:16), more fully to appreciate the all-illuminating light which, in Christ, 'was coming into the world' (Jn 1:9).

A notable 'greening' in Christian sensibilities and ecumenical commitments has resulted.[11] Indeed, Christian tradition has a great range of resources to bring to bear on environmental and ecological issues by drawing on its theological, moral, spiritual, philosophical,

---

8. Lynn White, 'The Historical Roots of our Ecological Crisis', in *Science* 155 (1967): 1203–7. For an apposite comment on White's influence, see Daniel Cowdin 'Environmental Ethics', in *Theological Studies* 69 (March 2008): 164–184, especially 165.

9. For example, Denis Edwards, *Ecology at the Heart of Faith* (Maryknoll, NY: Orbis, 2006), 2–4.

10. For notable further resource and a larger frame of reference, see *The Oxford Handbook of Religion and Ecology*, edited by Roger Gottlieb (New York: Oxford University Press, 2006).

11. For example, Ian Bradley, *God is Green: Christianity and the Environment* (London: Darton, Longman and Todd, 1990); and Rupert Sheldrake, *The Rebirth of Nature. The Greening of Science and God* (New York: Bantam Books, 1992); Sean McDonagh, *Greening the Christian Millennium* (Dublin: Dominican Publications, 1999); Roger Gottlieb, *A Greener Faith: Religious Environmentalism and Our Planet's Future* (New York: Oxford University Press, 2006).

and artistic experience, and by celebrating the goodness of creation as a whole, centred on the focal truth of the incarnation.[12] Then there are the larger dimensions of specifically human experience of special relevance in this critical moment. First, there is a sense of the immense, labouring fertility of the past which has brought us forth and placed us together in this present moment; and, secondly, a responsibility for the future which in some quite new way will be the product of our present decisions. A 'common era' has been forced upon us by the sheer extent of the ecological responsibilities we must now shoulder.

Effective organisation for the sake of the environment presupposes a large measure of community. Here, Christian *koinonia* is especially relevant for redefining the Church's ecumenical mission to the world and its search for new forms of planetary cooperation geared to the ecological well-being of the planet. There is no simple answer to be found by merely legislating for the structures necessary to maintain the quality of the biosphere. The deep values and meanings inspiring human life on planet earth cannot be produced by legal decree. Legislative bodies can change laws, but they cannot change hearts. The Church, however, is familiar with the great *oikumene* of religious faith. It cultivates a sense of the transcendent, the holy, the ultimately worthwhile. It thereby produces an energy powerful in its ability to sustain communities of meaning and moral action in the service of an integral ecology.

In this respect, Christian communities have both a redemptive and a constructive role. All forms of community are vulnerable to the baleful influence of 'the seven deadly sins': pride and greed, envy and apathy, violence, lust and dishonesty remain ever apt to frustrate the possibilities of collaboration in promoting the common good. For Christian faith, forgiveness and reconciliation

---

12. J Ronald Engel, 'The Ethics of Sustainable Development', in *Ethics of Environment and Development*, edited by I Robert Engel and Joan Gibb Engel (Tucson: University of Arizona Press, 1989), 13–15. Also James A Nash, *Loving Nature. Ecological Integrity and Christian Responsibility* (Nashville: Abingdon Press, 1991) is especially valuable in the section 'The Ecological Complaint against Christianity', 68–91.

remain real possibilities, no matter how godforsaken the historical situation seems to be, and whatever the extent of past failures and destructiveness. In that hope, the Church acts within culture by witnessing to God's limitless mercy. It encourages the integrity required to confess social sins for what they are, and to renew hope even when healing seems impossible. Without such honesty and hope, any culture is locked in an endless rationalising in regard to its deepest failures. A new beginning can be made. Hope inspires an imagination of the world 'otherwise', so that history is not the sum total of human failures and destructiveness, but ever-subject to a last word of grace and limitless mercy.

More positively still, the Church has a constructive role to play in the global and ecological turn in human consciousness. Christian faith is living familiarity with the universe as the one creation of God. The Spirit of God's self-giving love is the field of life-giving, transforming energy pervading all creation. In those who surrender to it, the Holy Spirit inspires a sense of the totality, a *uni-verse*, of all things in Christ, along with an outreach to the suffering other, in whatever form she or he (or it!) is present. Such faith traditionally celebrates the divine presence within creation in the sacramental forms of its worship. There the humble realities of our world become icons of the mystery at work.

The energies of Christian faith, then, offer deep resources for the development of a global and ecologically attuned consciousness. On the other hand, an ecumenical faith learns from the explorations of science and from the ethical concerns now stirring in human history. Further, discovering the riches of other religious faiths and traditions, the churches find themselves in a situation for which its central mysteries have been preparing it, and out of which it can contribute powerfully to the one, global human community. Faith and the love that informs it witness to transcendent beauty—the glory that has been revealed, yet too often remains concealed by excessive rationalism and moralising. A sense of the universe as God's creation inspires faith to ally itself with the world of art. Art is that domain of creativity by which our experience is freed and refreshed to perceive the original beauty—and even the beauty of the natural environment—that the pressures of life obscure and distort.[13]

This, then, is one way in which the community-forming mission of the Church operates within the planetary community. The Church is not a world to itself, for it is now both a teacher and a learner in a new situation. In its Greek roots, 'ecology' signifies 'the ordered meaning of the home'. It promises for Christian faith a new home-coming as it enters the doors of ecological awareness and concern. In this regard, it comes not as an alien intruder, but as a member of the whole human family, and as embodied in the interconnected, pluriform web of life of the planet itself. The Church necessarily views humanity as 'earthed' in the great temporal and spatial genesis of the cosmos itself. Christian humility deepens with the realisation of our inescapable dependence on a world of living and non-living things for our existence, nourishment and delight. There follows a fresh infusion of responsibility, too, with the recognition that it is given to human beings, for better or worse, deeply to affect the whole world of ecological existence. The fate of the planet and of future generations of all living things has come to depend on human decision. But there is also hope, too, since faith lives from the conviction that we are not alone in the universe. There is the *Other*, creatively, graciously present in its every moment.

A stunted inner environment prejudices any recognition of the wonder of life. We cannot go out of ourselves to the other—to God, neighbour and the world—if we are imprisoned in a self-centred existence. The psalms (for example, Ps 104; 136:6; 148:3–5) continually provoke faith into a movement of cosmic praise, and, in this way, anticipate, and even extend the scope of the Canticle of St Francis [72]. Likewise the prophets communicate a sense of God present in all creation and history (Isa 40:28f; Jer 32:17, 21). These sacred writings of Israel, including the books of Job and Wisdom [74], together inspire a great act of faith and hope: injustice and

---

13. For a discussion of beauty, Daniel Cowdin, 'Environmental Ethics', in *Theological Studies* 69 (March 2008): 174–178.

evil are not invincible, and the God who created the universe out of nothing can form in us a new mind and heart. The Spirit can inspire a new appreciation of the world both as the manifestation God and as home for all. Human beings do not have absolute power over creation. Indeed, to pretend to such power is the way of oppression and destruction [75]. Hence, care for nature, even to the point of protecting humanity from self-destruction [79] is integral to the mission of the Church. It witnesses God's transcendence to the world, the mystery within which all creation 'lives and moves and has its being' (Acts 17:28). The creative Spirit of God is working in and through all creation, inspiring the laborious growth of the world to maturity so that it can bring forth its best fruits. The God who fills the universe also fills it with possibilities. The new is always possible [80]. In that world of emerging possibilities, the human being has a creative role [81]. In the human mind and in the love of the human heart, the unfolding mystery of nature is illumined and directed. The human person is made for dialogue with the God who is present to all and in all, the creative source of all. We human beings must never consider ourselves as the centre, but as called to care for all God's creation, and to enjoy it as a gift [82].

The mark of the Church that is most characteristic of the ecumenical progress is catholicity. The Greek roots, *kat' holou*, suggest 'universal', 'all-embracing', 'in communion with the whole'. Whatever the position of particular Christian traditions—Catholic, Orthodox, Anglican, Protestant—catholicity is generally accepted as a mark of the authenticity for the community of faith and the ecclesial community professing the 'one, holy, catholic and apostolic' of the Nicene Creed. The feature of catholicity is today enjoying a larger application as it opens to an ecological and cosmic frame of reference, within the mystery of Christ 'in whom all things hold together' (Col 1:17). Simone Weil's question is pertinent, 'How can Christianity call itself Catholic if the universe is left out?', [14] or, we might add, 'if the earth and its diversity of life are ignored?'

---

14. Simone Weil, *Waiting for God* (London: Fontana, 1959), 116.

In other words, the ecology of life in Christ is at once a model and an inspiration of an ecology of love and care for the created world. Christian faith can contribute a sense of thanksgiving for all creation and reverence for all God's creatures in the light of Christ, and with the incarnational and sacramental awareness that flows from it. To adore the will of God means concern, in love and justice, for the neighbour and the neighbourhood, social and ecological. Further, because of the resurrection of the crucified, there is hope for all, despite the mortality and travail that are inescapably dimensions of earthly life.

6. The Gift

Culture cannot ignore nature, society cannot dismiss the personal uniqueness of each human being, the economy cannot ignore ecology, and the neighbour cannot be loved except though care of the environmental neighbourhood. Humanity exists within the interrelated wholeness of life. Valuing one's own body and sexual being is the condition for accepting the whole world as a gift within an integral human ecology [155]. The stifling self-absorption of modern anthropocentrism has dulled the capacity to receive life and existence as a gift, even to the point of demeaning the role of the human in the world of creation [115]. This is not to say that there are not real limits to human activity if its stewardship is to be responsible. Human beings can neither replace God, the Creator of all, nor dominate creation as if it were raw material for human purposes. Ignoring the most vulnerable in our midst—the disadvantaged, the poor, and even the unborn [120], is not a good beginning for hearing the cry of nature: the intimate interconnections of all in the mystery of life on this planet cannot be forgotten [117–118].

In the human mind and heart, the gift of life and the environment become known and loved; and the world itself appreciated in its every detail is an aspect of God's creative power and providence. When this sense of God-given gift is diminished, both the social and ecological networks of life are made vulnerable to an extreme anthropocentrism. Our vision must go beyond the calculus of economic advantage and continue to challenge the limits of flat, rationalistic analysis. In contrast, a deeply heartfelt sense of belonging to the created world cannot permit it, or any part of it, to be something owned and exploited for individual or group advantage [11–12]. Once an ecological conversion begins, harm to the environment, and the loss of particular species, strike home, to be experienced by many as a form of personal suffering [19, 89]. Ecological conversion, in the words of the prophet, means to find that 'the heart of stone' can be replaced by 'the heart of flesh' (Ezek 36:26)—compassionately alive to the whole world of nature and life on this planet.

Admittedly, the obsessions and compulsions of consumerist culture—'the heart of stone'—do not readily yield to Ezechiel's 'heart of flesh'. To the degree society becomes 'a seedbed for collective selfishness' [145], ecological conversion and the recognition of the gift and beauty of creation can seem a sentimental and impractical indulgence. In today's world, the earth is subject to rapid changes [17–19), and industrial production increasingly depends on non-renewable resources, [20–22]. But a throw-away culture increases the garbage to be dealt with [204]. The emptier the heart—in the coldness and unfeeling of the 'heart of stone'—the more one is driven to buy, possess and consume. Talk of the common good becomes an empty rhetorical flourish [182]. What is needed, therefore, before embarking on new industrial ventures, is an assessment of the likely environmental impact before any project proceeds. Consequently, an integral ecology favours co-ordinated planning for the preservation of the natural environment over episodic intervention on behalf of endangered species of fauna or flora, for this can be too little and too late [184].

When huge environmental issues need to be faced with clarity and energy, physical and mental pollution do not inspire either responsibility or creativity. Relentless advertising in the mass media 'mediates' the world to our minds and hearts, colonising the imagination with consumer-driven concerns. In that world of endless and artificial neediness, there is no joy in life and no room for receiving it, and the whole of creation, as a gift. The modern mind is burdened with forms of overload, both in terms of information and responsibility. The needs are too great, the perceived failures so immense, that narcotic dependence becomes for many, even the young, the only possibility of relief. It is possible that the present situation lacks the resources—cultural, economic, political and religious—to confront the crisis that is upon us [53]. When cultural resources are so drastically diminished, the most powerful force is the market [56]. It becomes the ultimate criterion [123], to the point where more humane considerations are impossible. Well-intended laws look like arbitrary impositions on a freedom without cultural virtues. Admittedly, virtues and good dispositions without laws lack social effectiveness. The only way forward is to foster dialogue in the interests of a comprehensive solution: neither oppressive technocracy nor antihuman ideology—nor, for that matter, an unearthly religiosity—can offer any solution.

7. Human Nature in the Natural World

The natural law of integral ecology is not an external abstract norm. It is based in living intelligence and moral consciousness present to the other, in a heart-to-heart, eye-to-eye, mind-to-mind acknowledgement of all others as partners in an enterprise of global ecological responsibility. How does evolutionary emergence, however, affect a notion of integral ecology? Intense emphasis on the ethical might well make us oblivious of the generic 'animality' of the human condition. Here, socio-biology, when detached from its ideologies, can teach us much about human behaviour by setting humanity within the evolutionary emergence of the animal. By recovering the 'animal' within us, we more adequately understand ourselves. The details are subject, of course, to wide ranging debate. But balanced perceptions are beginning to emerge. We are not 'disembodied intelligences tentatively considering possible incarnations', but concretely embodied human beings with 'highly particular, sharply limited needs and possibilities'.[15] Our capacities

---

15. Mary Midgley, *Beast and Man: The Biological Roots of Human Nature* (Ithaca: Cornell

to bond, to care for our young, to feel for the whole group are rooted in our evolutionary animal nature. As Mary Midgley observes, 'We are not just like animals; we *are* animals'.[16] By accepting our animality, we can counter anthropocentrism and the tendency to think of ourselves as a detached intelligence, living in an isolated, self-sufficient individuality, jealously asserting one's own rights against all others. Our kinship with the animal realm counters any ethereal sentimentality in regard to both individual existence and global belonging. Particular feelings and actual bondings are 'given' in ways that demand to be respected. Neither interpersonal relations nor religiously-inspired universal love can afford to bypass a natural ordering of relationships.[17]

By owning our place in an evolutionary biological world, we will be less inclined to think of the human self as a free-floating consciousness. Our present responsibilities have a biologically-based emotional constitution. They are shaped in a particular direction by the genesis of nature. There are 'givens' in the human constitution; and these conditions precede freedom, never to be repudiated unless at the cost of denaturing ourselves in a fundamental manner. In sexuality, for instance, neither culture, nor a person-centred spirituality, is the only consideration.

Primary relationships to family, friends, community, society, land and region need to be recognised in their particularity as priorities in human concerns. We belong to the whole human family through a particular family. We enter the global community by being connected to a special place and time. Openness to all is possible only by way of the given limits.

Still, our genetic emergence provides a basis for a deep sympathy, in the strongest sense of the word, with the whole community of living things. The other is not first of all a rival or a client, nor a possession or a resource, but a companion in the unique community of life on this planet: 'We are incurably members of one another' [18].

University, 1978) 71.

16. Midgley, Beast and Man, xiii.

17. See Stephen J Pope, 'The Order of Love and Recent Catholic Ethics: A Constructive Proposal', in *Theological Studies* 52/2, (June, 1991): 255288.

18. Mary Midgley, *Animals and Why They Matter* (New York: Penguin, 1983), 21.

In short, human history cannot cut itself off from nature, nor is it natural for nature to swallow up human history in meaninglessness, to wipe the screen clean of human meaning in blank extinction. One cannot easily believe that evolution aims at decapitation. Yet neither does it aim at disembodiment. The historical challenge at the moment is to achieve a new embodiment, a new earthing in the planetary and cosmic process, a full-bodied recognition of the past within the wholeness of the history and nature that has brought us forth.

Integral ecology, ordered to the common good of all, becomes more differentiated in the light of new responsibilities. The complete hierarchy of values—for example, physical, chemical, biological, ecological, economic, political, social, cultural and religious constituents of our global humanity—must be acknowledged. There can be no adequate response to complex questions dealing with the bio-physical environment unless it includes the moral ecology of values which sustain human culture in its varied responsibilities to the ecology of the biosphere of nature itself. In recent centuries, the destruction to the biosphere, and the resultant threat to its myriad species, has been of appalling proportions. Hence, an integral ecology will insist on linking human culture to the biophysical milieu in which it is embodied and sustained. Though human consciousness transcends the immediate bio-physical environment, it does so only by accepting its specific responsibility for the natural world, and living in harmony with it. The extent of human destructiveness in this respect underlines the need for some kind of ecology of the values within human consciousness itself if it is to be formed into a responsible care for the biophysical reality of the environment. The self-transcending, other-directness which is the basic law of individuals and communities, is not motivated by some abstract Platonic ideal. It is related to this natural world, as it exists on this small planet. Human beings do not haunt the world in a detached impersonal analysis, but inhabit it as a homeland and a neighbourhood in which all life is respected.

The various cultural and religious resources [63] found in art, literature, sacred writings, liturgical action and mystical contemplation, contribute to the ecological commitment which is intrinsic to faith [64]. The Creation accounts in the Bible bring together relationships to God, the neighbour and to the earth [66], together with the principle of common ownership. All this requires that human intelligence respect the particular nature of things. Each living being has a value in God's eyes, which counts more than pragmatic usefulness. There is a larger world of wonder overflowing the limited scope of mere human utility. In that perspective of one divine creation, everything is interconnected [70]

7. The Milieu of Christ

As the focus of Christian faith, the risen and ascended Christ is not contained by creation, but himself already contains and fills the universe [83]: all things are made through him and for him and in him, for he is the first born from the dead, the one in whom the frailties of creation have been overcome and brought to their fulfilment. In him, each being sings the hymn of its existence [85], just as every aspect of creation reveals the creative love of God. The whole of nature is the locus of God's presence [88, 96]. Through the incarnation of the Word [99], God has claimed the world as his own. God is present from the beginning, and is ever-present in a hidden manner within the natural world. The risen Christ is in all things, drawing them to their fulfilment [100, 221]. The image of the Lamb slain before the foundation of the world (Rev 13:8) reveals that creation has arisen from an unimaginable self-giving on the part of God at every moment. No matter what the evil and the agony distorting this good creation, the loving sacrifice of the God who so loved the world as to give his only Son, promises a healing and mercy that will triumph over all evil.

Though there can be no pantheistic confusion of God and creation, for the Creator and creatures are interrelated in a 'sublime communion' [89]. All created things exist in mutual dependence and service, to the praise of the creator. In this relationship, the earth is not divinised, nor is the wondrous variety of life-forms unrecognised, just as the human retains a unique position within the whole. [90]. Life is enriched in loving the neighbour, especially the poorest, and loving the ecological neighbourhood, especially in regard to the species that are most endangered [91].

An integral ecology presupposes the integrity of a deep spirituality drawing on the ever-renewable resources of the Spirit. It also demands the creativity of work, as in the Benedictine motto, *ora et labora*. When informed by an attitude of receptivity and gratitude work is not a soul-less activity, nor the manifestation of the greed that seeks personal gain to the exclusion of all else. According to their different capacities in prayer, science and action, all can contribute to the social capital on which to draw in a situation of ecological crisis [128]. The rich heritage of Christian spirituality, the fruit of twenty centuries of personal and communal experience, has a precious contribution to make to the renewal of humanity in this critical period [216].

Pope Benedict observed that 'the external deserts in the world are growing, because the internal deserts have become so vast' [152]. For this reason, the ecological crisis is also a summons to profound interior conversion. An 'ecological conversion' is needed, inspired and sustained by Christian faith. An essential aspect of the Christian vocation is to respect, protect and develop the whole environment of God's creation. Christian life unfolds in gratitude for all God's loving gift, in an awareness of participating in a great communion of life and interdependence [220]. Each created reality reflects something of God and is contained in Christ. By being present to each reality and to each moment in creation, we live in ever greater horizons of understanding and hope in anticipation of life to the full [223]. Such hopes call for deep humility in adoration and praise of the Creator. To lose such humility inevitably ends up harming society and the environment [224]. On the other hand, care for nature is part of a lifestyle which includes the capacity of living together in interpersonal communion. Jesus reminds us that having

God as our common Father makes us all brothers and sisters—even to the point of loving our enemies and accepting the forces of nature in universal fraternity [228].

Love for all and everything in God must inform every action that seeks to build a better world, even in the 'macro-relationships, social, economic and political . . . . [231]: In order to make society more human, more worthy of the human person, the value of love in social life—political, economic and cultural—must be appreciated as the highest norm for all activity' [157]. Such love informs integral ecology and motivates ecological conversion.

These seven perspectives on the Encyclical put us in the position to explore the particular spiritual and theological issues entailed in an integral ecology. It involves 'a new synthesis' for humanity in the world of today and its complex challenges. Catholic tradition handled the inevitable complexities in the earthly experience of life and death by making distinctions between grace and nature (with grace healing and perfecting nature), a strong theology of creation and God's universal presence, and by respecting the different but analogically related domains of faith and reason, along with perennial explorations of natural law in various contexts of individual and social morality. In all this, the Incarnation was an implicit but fundamental consideration, and the sacraments of the Church deriving from it. In such a differentiated context, the Church exercises its teaching mission to the world. Clearly, an integral ecology, with its new synthesis [63], is called on to focus these various elements in its tradition on the concrete reality of the earth, the locus of the incarnation, and the continuing gift of God to all as we care for 'our common home'. Many questions arise, and many particular topics call for further exploration. The first of these is creation itself.

2

Creator, Creation and Ecology

In his concern for the environmental crisis, Pope Francis wrote, 'Unless we struggle with these deeper issues, I do not believe that our concern for ecology will produce significant results' [160]. The 'deeper issue' in the context concerns the meaning of life, existence and our work in the world. Of radical relevance are the mystery of creation and the character of the Creator, for these affect our sense of reality, human, environmental and cosmic. The words of Pope Francis suggest the direction this reflection will take:

> In the Judaeo-Christian tradition, the word 'creation' has a broader meaning than 'nature', for it has to do with God's loving plan in which every creature has its own value and significance. Nature is usually seen as a system which can be studied, understood and controlled, whereas creation can only be understood as a gift from the outstretched hand of the Father of all, and as a reality illuminated by the love which calls us together into universal communion [76].

Accordingly, this reflection is presented under three headings:

1. The meaning of Creation
2. The character of the Creator
3. A changed understanding of the world

1. The Meaning of Creation

Central to the biblical tradition, are creation accounts in Genesis (Gen 1:1–2:3; Gen 2:4–24).[1] They represent a marvellous morning dream of the universe as God's original gift. The world appears as an ordered and differentiated whole. Human beings are introduced into such a totality to share in God's own creativity through responsibility and care. Within such a world, the human community will find nothing to equal God, for God is the world-originating source of all good. Though evil, suggested by the serpent in the garden, has its opaque presence in human experience, it is not from God; evil is from creatures gone wrong; it is the perversion of creation, neither its original nor final condition. In every reality, and behind every moment of history, is the utterly free and unconditioned power of divine creativity. In Deutero-Isaiah (Isa 40–66), the great theme of God as Creator is employed to bolster the hopes of Israel in its experience of captivity. God can bring about a new exodus.

The sense of creation that Christianity inherits from Israel would be truncated if no mention were made of the more immanent, participative emphasis evident in the Wisdom literature. It contrasts with the rather ordered pictorial accounts characteristic of Genesis. The feminine character of creative wisdom is to the forefront, as the divine presence pervades and encompasses all experience. To give one example,

> . . . for wisdom the fashioner of all things taught me. There is in her a spirit that is intelligent, holy, unique, manifold, subtle, mobile, clear, unpolluted, distinct, invulnerable, loving the good, keen, irresistible, humane, steadfast, sure, free from anxiety, all-powerful, overseeing all and penetrating through all spirits that are intelligent, pure and altogether subtle . . . she is the breath of the power of God and a pure emanation of the glory of the Almighty (Wis 7:22–25).

---

1.   The act of God in calling things into existence, as expressed in the Hebrew term, *bárá*.

Divine wisdom moves in and through the 'all things' as an attractive, all-pervasive, life-giving reality (Prov 8:22–9:6; Sir 1:1-20; 24:1-22; Wis 7:22–9:18; Eph 4:6). In this, we have an indication of Israel's true *philosophia*, the 'love of wisdom'—and of what, for us today, most inspires and sustains an integral ecology—and which carries over into the New Testament in the key texts of John 1:1–18, Romans 8:18–25, Ephesians 1:3-23, and Colossians 1:15–20.

In the history of Christian thinking, there are two names deserving special mention for their understanding of the world of creation, and the place of the human within it: Maximus Confessor and St Thomas Aquinas.

The great saint of East and West, Maximus Confessor (580–662), understood the role of humanity within the cosmos of creation, and so, anticipates the 'integral ecology' that is our concern. He writes,

> . . . the human person which is *the laboratory in which everything is concentrated* and itself naturally *mediates between the extremities of each division*, having been drawn into everything in a good and fitting way through becoming . . . [Difficulty 41:1305B][2]

In his emphasis on the multi-relational character of the human existence, Maximus exploits the Platonic idea, as found in *Timaeus*), of the human being as a microcosm of the cosmic totality, so that the human is the 'laboratory' in which the variety of our manifold experience of creation worked out. For Maximus the human is something of a cosmic crossroads of all elements of creation, a natural bonding of the universe. Basic to Maximus theological emphasis are the memorable words of St Gregory Nazianzen on the Feast of the Epiphany/Theophany,now incorporated in liturgies of East and West: 'a marvelous mystery is proclaimed today: natures are instituted afresh, and God becomes man'(*Mirabile mysterium declaratur hodie; innovantur naturae; Deus homo factus est*).

---

2. See Andrew Louth, *Maximus The Confessor* (London: Routledge, 1996), 32–3. I am relying on Louth's translation.

The human is involved in the complexity and separations that are inherent to the structure of creation, to become, as it were, a channel of communication and reconciliation within that world of divisions. Thus, the *logos* of specific nature of human being is characterised by a process of becoming, of reaching beyond its present state, in the direction of what is other, for the sake of wholeness, unity and communion. In this, the human is an agent of the divine purpose, indeed of the divine *Logos* in which the coherence and goal of creation is found. The human being 'can come to be a way of fulfilment for what is divided' and be shown forth as the bearer of 'the great mystery of divine purpose'. Thus, it participates in God's creative providence (Diff 10:1189A–B), to be 'the natural bond mediating between the universal poles'. In the human, the disparate and the divided are brought into unity, and isolation is uniquely overcome.

After evoking something of the wisdom of Maximus in the context of the challenges facing us today in terms of an integral ecology, we now turn to the writings of St Thomas Aquinas.

In *Summa Contra Gentiles*,[3] Aquinas, heir as he is to the patristic inheritance, asks whether the consideration of creatures is useful for the enlightenment of faith. His positive answer reveals a sturdy and reverent realism. Creatures in all their variety image forth God in some way, and lead to an appreciation of the divine wisdom, and witness to the manifold creativity of God's power. Further, the beauty and delicacy of the created world ignites in the human mind a love for the divine goodness from which created realities derive. In this contemplation of the creator, human beings achieve in themselves 'a certain likeness to the divine perfection and wisdom'. The human mind and heart begins to participate in God's own self-knowledge and love, and thereby share in God's own awareness of the created world as manifesting the divine perfections.[4]

> . . . the consideration of creation sparks in the human
> soul a love for the divine goodness. Whatever goodness

---

3.   Thomas Aquinas, *Summa contra Gentiles*, l. 2, c. 2 (SCG).
4.   Aquinas, SCG, l. 2, c. 45.

and perfection is spread out in different creatures, it is a totality brought wholly together in him as in the source of all goodness . . . If therefore the goodness, the beauty and the delicacy [literally, *suavitas*] of creatures so lures the human soul, the source-good of God himself, diligently compared to the streams of goodness in the variety of creatures, inflames and attracts totally to itself our human souls.[5]

The divine mystery is thus experienced in creation as an attractive force within a 'sublime' communion [89] progressively luring human consciousness into the experience of original goodness that God is. In this tradition, Pope Francis writes,

The universe did not emerge as the result of arbitrary omnipotence, a show of force or a desire for self-assertion. Creation is of the order of love. God's love is the fundamental moving force in all created things: 'For you love all things that exist, and detest none of the things that you have made; for you would not have made anything if you had hated it' (Wis 11:24) [77].

A further consideration appeals to a more intimate sense of participation in the divine. By considering the variety of creation, we human beings achieve in ourselves 'a certain likeness to the divine perfection and wisdom'. Since God knows (and loves) everything in himself, and as we human beings participate in God's self-knowledge and love through faith, we begin to share in the divine consciousness of creation. To illustrate this luminous new consciousness of creation, Aquinas goes on to quote St Paul, 'And all of us, with unveiled faces, seeing the glory of the Lord . . . are being transformed into the same image . . . ' (2 Cor 3:18).

The created world is here appreciated as the manifestation of the Creator and as drawing us to participate in God's own creative

---

5.   SCC, l.2, c. 45.

wisdom. Such a vision can inspire a contemporary ecological and cosmically attuned theology. On the other hand, there can be no question of confusing creation or nature with God. In fact, Thomas goes on to say that the proper appreciation of creation is necessary, not only for finding truth but also for excluding errors.[6] As we intelligently search through the world of creation, we find that no creature is independent in its existence, and that no element of our world is 'the first cause' of everything. We must learn to value the variety of created realities within the englobing mystery of existence, and receive it all as a gift. According to this medieval vision, the variety of creation radiates from the one inexhaustible divine origin:

> God is . . . the most perfect agent. Therefore, it belongs to him to induce his image in created things in the most perfect way in a manner that befits created nature. But created things cannot attain to the perfect image of God in a single form: the cause exceeds the effect. For what exists in the cause in utter simplicity, is realised in the effect in a composite and pluriform manner . . . It is fitting, then, that there be a multiplicity and variety in created things so that God's image be found in them perfectly in accord with their mode of being.[7]

In Aquinas' theology, we find a wisdom that deeply appreciates the variety and precious particularities of creation. Each element of creation has its own quasi-absolute value. It is a particular realisation of the divine [33]. The numinous sense of nature that so many ecologists bring to their commitments today is no doubt living from a subterranean connection with this great medieval vision:

> God planned to create many distinct things in order to share with them and reproduce in them his goodness. Because no one creature could do this, he produced

---

6.   *SCG*, l. 2, c. 3.
7.   *SCG*, l. 2, c. 45.

many diverse creatures, so that what was lacking in one expression of his goodness could be made up by another; for the goodness which is simply and wholly in God, is shared in by creatures in many different ways. Hence, the whole universe shares and expresses that goodness better than any individual creature.[8]

And yet there is a further point, too often overlooked, in this classic sense of creation. The mystery of creation, in its variety and unity, not only shares in the beauty and goodness of the Creator. The universe is brought into existence by an act of free creative love.[9] The being and variety of creation is total gift. God's love is not first attracted toward something already existing. Rather, everything, inasmuch as it exists, has been loved into existence by the divine freedom: *amor Dei infundens et creans bonitatem in rebus*. Creation, from this point of view, is enacted as a communication of the divine joy in the existence of what is other. It is sheer gift. The patristic and medieval tradition speaks of the ultimate Good as diffusive of itself (*Bonum est diffusivum sui*). The universe, therefore, is a divinely chosen order of being, and not a kind of necessary emanation from, or completion of, a remote deity. In all its variety and connectedness, the created universe is a communication from the heart of God. As the encyclical has it,

> The universe unfolds in God, who fills it completely. Hence, there is a mystical meaning to be found in a leaf, in a mountain trail, in a dewdrop, in a poor person's face. The ideal is also to discover God in all things. Saint Bonaventure teaches us that 'contemplation deepens the more we feel the working of God's grace within our hearts, and the better we learn to encounter God in creatures outside ourselves' [233].

---

8. *STh* I, q. 47, a. 1.
9. *STh* I, q. 20. a. 2.

And from a footnote,

> The spiritual writer Ali al-Khawas stresses from his own experience the need not to put too much distance between the creatures of the world and the interior experience of God. As he puts it: 'Prejudice should not have us criticize those who seek ecstasy in music or poetry. There is a subtle mystery in each of the movements and sounds of this world. The initiate will capture what is being said when the wind blows, the trees sway, water flows, flies buzz, doors creak, birds sing, or in the sound of strings or flutes, the sighs of the sick, the groans of the afflicted . . .' [10] [233].

A number of valuable points stand out:

1. 'The universe unfolds in God who fills it completely' [233].
2. 'Hence, there is a mystical meaning to be found in a leaf, in a mountain trail, in a dewdrop, in a poor person's face'. The mystical meaning in question is not an unreal construction, but the result of a deep contemplation of reality itself
3. Saint Bonaventure, referred to above, teaches us that 'contemplation deepens the more we feel the working of God's grace within our hearts, and the better we learn to encounter God in creatures outside ourselves'. This is not merely a feeling, but an insight and a contact. The more grace of God moves us, the more we see a universe of grace, and God present in all things.

---

10. The encyclical is quoting *Anthologie du soufisme*, edited by Eva de Vitray-Meyerovitch (Paris, 1978), 200, footnote 159.

4. The ninth century spiritual Sufi writer Ali al-Khawas stresses from his own experience the need not to put too much distance between the creatures of the world and the interior experience of God.

The stable world of particular natures linked in a great chain of being is as it envisaged in the medieval vision differs from the evolving universe as it is appears today. In contemporary thinking, the whole is a process before it is an ordered collection of particular natures. But here, I think, two remarks might be made. First, Aquinas exhibits a serene delight in the specific value of each element of creation as loved into being. Each being serves to manifest the divine goodness in a particular way. To that degree, such a vision mitigates the cosmic sadness of an uncritical evolutionary myth which can read like an obituary for the casualties of evolution. The fittest survived; the weakest did not; and even what survives is subjected to the blind, harsh law that values only the present. In contrast, the medieval vision, even while it leaves unknown the mysterious ways of Providence, finds an existential value in things simply because they exist—or existed in a certain way at a certain time. It is a reminder to those who would hurry to frame the laws of evolution to take into account two considerations. First, each individual entity is a world of mystery in the sheer fact of its existence. Before it can be considered a link in the chain of evolution, or as an aspect of the larger emerging complexity, it is, or was, *there*! The evolutionary potential—or lack of it—of the *Marella splendens*, or of any of eighty thousand extraordinarily complex creatures unearthed in the Burgess Shale in Western Canada, does not evacuate the fundamental wonder of its existence in the play and contingency of what happened in time.[11] The unique existence of the individual entity is so often 'the missing link' in evolutionary

---

11. Apart from an abundance of exciting documentation and marvellous instances of the variety of the past, Stephen Jay Goulding, *Wonderful Life. The Burgess Shale and the Nature of History* (London: Penguin, 1989) is a striking model of scientific reconstruction, even as it poses profound philosophical questions.

thinking. Secondly, the seemingly purposeless variety of what once existed or is existing in its unique manner should make us wary of any premature closure on the whole story of what is going on. The human mind is not a detached spectator, but is part of the emerging process. Our reconstructions and extrapolations, whatever the progress of science, access only fragments of the meaning of the whole process. The Thomistic emphasis on the necessary plurality of creation and on the value of each existent not only contests the simplicity of evolutionary myths, but serves to keep evolutionary theory attentive to a truly inclusive wholeness.[12] The system must remain open. The full story awaits, in patience and tentative exploration, the full understanding of creation that resides only in God.

Today's evolutionary worldview reveals limitations in the medieval view of the universe of stable and ordered natures. For the good that God is creating is not yet fully realised. The whole 'groaning' (Rom 8:18–28) totality of creation is awaiting its liberation. Our human role places us in creation as free agents, called to collaborate with the divine creative energy at work. Human freedom is not in competition with God, but God's gift to the created and evolving world. Human history is destined to work with God to bring about a good that is still emerging. As human existence participates in the divine knowledge and love, it contributes to the construction of a good world.[13] In this perspective, human freedom not only bears the guilty burden of appalling destructiveness; it is the condition of the good, the happy outcome, the efflorescence of love in the final ecology of the world.

While so much has changed with the expansion of scientific knowledge, it is worth recalling in the present context that, in the biblical vision of creation, the existence of other and higher forms of life was presumed. Their presence is now largely mediated to faith in the various liturgical prefaces in which the assembly is invited to join with "angels and archangels, cherubim and seraphim" in

---

12. See Celia Deane-Drummond, *The Wisdom of the Liminal; evolution and Other Animal in Human Becoming* (Grand Rapids, Michigan: Eerdmans, 2014).

13. F Stefano, 'The Evolutionary Categories of Juan Luis Segundo's Theology of Grace', in *Horizons* 19/1 (Spring 1992): 9.

a cosmic hymn of praise. At least to evoke that largely forgotten biblical dimension of the cosmos and to appropriate in whatever way the liturgical vision of creation suggests a more wonderful view of the living universe than that afforded by a flat, materialist anthropocentrism. The cosmic feelings and symbols of solidarity with all that is both below and above our form of life cannot but promote a greater awe and fresh questioning in the presence of so much that is still unknown. While the realm of created supra-human intelligence is largely ignored in current preoccupations, it still has a suggestive power. It functions as a symbol, to say the very least, of dimensions of reality that have yet to be considered in our efforts to understand the commonwealth of life and the community of consciousness in the universe of our present perceptions.[14]

2. The Creator

For the believer, the first and fundamental notion of God, the Creator of all, is found in an orientation to that limitless, living fullness of being and goodness which, alone, in the deepest sense of the traditional term, 'saves our souls' and gives us the universe, the One in whom we live and move and have our being. The character of God is, as it were, progressively anticipated in our search for ultimate, for the meaning of all we find meaningful, for the explanation of all our explanations. The attractiveness of God comes home to us in the beauty that draws us, and in all we experience as love and mercy, so as to reach beyond ourselves and our world, and upward to what the world cannot give. Faith recognises that God is not indifferent to our seeking, but is revealed in the words of the prophets, in the wisdom of the holy ones, in the word of sacred scriptures, in the inspiration of the Spirit and in the coming of Christ. The reality of God is tasted in the tang of life itself and touched in the wonder of each living thing. God is the giver of all good gifts, experienced as

---

14. For an inspiring Orthodox view of Vladimir Solovyov, see *A Solovyov Anthology*, edited by SL Frank (London: The Saint Austin Press, 2001), 127–138; likewise, drawing on Eastern Christian sources such as St Ephrem, Ps Dionysius and Armenian hymns, Vigan Guroian, *The Fragrance of God* (Grand Rapids: Eerdmans, 2006).

the all-creating and all-welcoming Love moving the universe to its fulfilment. To cite *Laudato Si'*,

> [Saint John of the Cross taught that all the goodness present in the realities and experiences of this world 'is present in God eminently and infinitely, or more properly, in each of these sublime realities is God'.
> This is not because the finite things of this world are really divine, but because the mystic experiences the intimate connection between God and all beings, and thus feels that 'all things are God [234].

The following points bear emphasizing:

1. All the goodness that is encountered and enjoyed is in God in its infinite form;

2. God is present in the depths of what we most experience as good;

3. While there can be no pantheistic confusion of God with the world, the contemplative can be so attuned to the creative presence of God in everything, that in the words of the Spiritual Canticle, all things 'are God'. This is another bold phrase and sounds similar to the pantheism the encyclical has already rejected. The point, rather, in the mind of the great spiritual writers and theologians is that everything that is, in its unique existence, mediates something of the infinite creative source from which it has emerged.

4. The anticipatory, ongoing character of the way we mean God makes dialogue possible with the reverently agnostic, be they scientists or meditative searchers. It is worth bearing in mind, in recognition of healthy biblical agnosticism, that God is not yet seen face to face, that God 'no one has ever seen' (Jn 1:18). Even though God is, for believers, the object

of love and faith and hope, the mystery is disclosed only in a progressive darkness.[15] Faith is the freedom to surrender to the original and ultimate mystery so as neither to grasp or contain it.

Thinking about divine creation points to a background theme in which all kinds of human creativity can improvise their variations as parts in the symphony of reality. We are taken closer to the nub of the contemporary question of creation in the following marvellous passage. Here, the biblical sage reflects on less conclusive kinds of wisdom:

> . . . they were unable from the good things that are seen to know the one who exists, nor did they recognise the artisan while paying heed to his works; but they supposed that either fire or wind or swift air or the circle of the stars, or turbulent water or the luminaries of heaven were gods that rule the world. If through delight in the beauty of these things people assumed them to be gods, let them know how much better than these things is their Lord, for the author of beauty created them. And if people were amazed at their power and working, let them perceive from them how much more powerful is the one who formed them. For from the greatness and beauty of created things comes a corresponding perception of their creator. Yet these people are little to be blamed, for perhaps they go astray while seeking God and desiring to find him. For while they live among his works, they keep searching, and they trust in what they see, because the things that are seen are beautiful. Yet again, not even they are to be excused; for if they had the power to know so much that they could investigate the world, how did they fail to find sooner the Lord of these things? (Wis 13:1–9).

---

15. See Thomas Aquinas, *STh*, I, q. 12, a. 13, ad 1: '. . . we are united to God as to one unknown'.

Today 'the good things that are seen' have been immeasurably extended. The magnitude of the energies and the infinitesimal intricacies of pattern and design are so fascinating, and so subversive of former visions of reality, that scientific language verges on the religious and the poetic in its effort to express the numinous value of the cosmos it celebrates. For on a purely scientific level a new enchantment with the beauty and wonder of the cosmos is apparent. Little wonder that there are those who feel they have discovered 'the gods that rule the world'. In comparison, the God of traditional faith seems little more than a naive projection.

The biblical sage graciously admits that those who confuse the wonders of creation with the wonder of the Creator are 'little to be blamed'. If the real wonders of the world inspire confidence in the beauty, complexity and sheer uncanniness of it all, it is likely that the search will continue for the full mystery intimated in such experience.

And yet there remains the possibility of stopping short of an integral ecology: '. . . how did they fail to find sooner the Lord of all things?' Admittedly, there is a certain limitation in searching for God without considering love, death, values, ethics, art, grace or the possibilities of divine self-revelation. Then, too, there is the problem of evil. The mind of God cannot be explored with profit if the mind of the explorer is inured to the drama and struggle for real life. But it need not be so. The very fact that so much of the cosmos is found to be profoundly intelligible and so elegantly beautiful, luminous with that *splendor entis*, that 'radiance of being' of which Aquinas speaks, invites the mind into its ultimate adventure: an exploration of the original mystery of it all. There is a beautiful expression of medieval wisdom: 'Creatures, as far as in them lies, do not turn us away from God but lead to God. If they do turn us away . . . that is due to those who, through their own fault, use them in ways that are contrary to reason'.[16]

We find ourselves in a new historical context affected by new scientific methods. Scientific research into ecology is, of course,

---

16. Thomas Aquinas, *STh* I, q. 65, a. 3.

like any other kind of human knowing. It deals with a specialised band of data, forms it into imaginative models, locates its questions in a world of meaning, weighs the evidence for the most probable position, and seeks applications of its findings in accord with a certain scale of values.

It is the same in our attempts to contribute to an integral ecology. The emphasis on the *integral* allows for further kinds of data. For example, a reflective faith explores the data of religious experience throughout history, above all, that expressed in the Scriptures and in the authoritative doctrinal formulations of the Councils. Theologians, for their part, formulate a doctrine of creation out of a radical, continuing demand to understand what has been revealed and witnessed to. As faith seeks further understanding, it can never pretend to the possession of some final answer, as though the mystery of God were fully comprehended. It is part of the wisdom of a searching faith to know its limits, even as it experiences the continuing force of questions regarding the meaning and applicability of what is held by faith, and, and even though the ultimate answer remains locked in silence and darkness.

3. A changed understanding of the world

A sense of creation today has to include new data in its vision, hitherto not only inaccessible but unimaginable in the past.[17] The psalmist of old saw, 'the heavens declare the glory of God, and the firmament shows forth his handiwork' (Ps 19:1). Likewise, the Psalmist praises the glory of God revealed in in the world of nature (Ps 136:6; 148:3–5; the Canticle of Daniel in Dan 3:57–88). The might of thunderstorms, the light of the sun and moon, the twinkling stars, the steady glow of the planets, the shimmering Milky Way, the birds of the skies, animals wild and tame, the fish of the sea and monsters of the deep, the trees and flowers and produced of the land, all draw us to praise the creator. These, however, are only a tiny fraction of

---

17.   John F Haught, *Christianity and Science: Toward a Theology of Nature* (Maryknoll, NY: Orbis, 2007) is a valuable reference.

the realities that intrigue our minds today. For instance, today the glory of the heavens includes the icy rings encircling Saturn, the satellites of Neptune, the delicate blue of the earth seen from the moon, our 100 billion sun galaxy in a universe of perhaps a one hundred billion galaxies. Our telescopes and computations extend to the ultra-energetic quasars, to explosive enormous supernovas, even to the space-time rifts of 'black holes'. We know, too, that a million earths could be hidden in the sun; that light blazing through space at 300,000 km per second takes 100,000 years just to span our particular galaxy. Though Alpha Centuri is our nearest star, it is still four light years away. We have wonderful photographs of distant objects such as the Ant Nebula, and that is over three thousand light years away? From the quark, with its variations, to the quasar, it is a universe of incredible proportions. And then, the ecological sciences of our time can explore the hundreds of thousands of species of living things that now populate this planet, and catalogue the fossils of those that once lived, and, at the same time, record a list of the species that are now endangered.

Today's sense, not only of the immense variety of planetary life but also of the immeasurably great and the immeasurably small dimensions of physical matter, has to reach back to hitherto unimaginable expanses of time; and within that time, the evolutionary dynamics that have produced this world of life. Human consciousness, trembling before the uncanny extent of the 14.7 billion year history of this universe, comes to realise that these thousands of millions of years are the past from which we human beings emerged in the uncanny contingencies of what actually happened. In the first few seconds of this 15 billion year-old universe, there appeared all the fundamental particles and constants without which life on this seemingly insignificant little planet would have been impossible.[18] The velocity of light, the charge on the electron, the mass of the proton, the constant emissions of energy, are exactly what they should have been if life were to teem in all its forms on earth. A slight difference

---

18. For a fuller discussion, John Polkinghorne, *Quarks, Chaos and Christianity. Questions to Science and Religion* (New York: Crossroad, 2000).

then would have meant no life now. If the charge on the electron had been slightly different, if the reaction between two protons had been slightly different, if the force of gravity had been slightly different, then the universe as we know it, would never have come to be. All those millions of hydrogen atoms formed billions years ago, which today in various combinations make up the composition of the human body, would have turned into the inert gas, helium. There would have been no water, no life, no human beings..[19] In his *A Brief History of Time*,[20] Stephen Hawking estimates that if the rate of the expansion of the universe one second after the Big Bang had been smaller even one part in a hundred thousand million, the whole would have collapsed before it reached its present size.[21] But if the rate of expansion had been greater, the universe would have become an enormous bubble of gas blown out too quickly to allow the stars to form. And if there were no stars, there could be no formation of the heavy elements that are essential for the biological processes characteristic of this planet. If the four forces shaping the cosmos had been stronger or weaker in any way,[22] there would be no carbon, no hydrogen, no water, and none of the heavy elements to be the raw materials for life's emergence. Then, too, the force of gravity holds all physical entities together in fields of mutual attraction. If that had been different, the other forces would have acted in different ways, and the present happy outcome would have been precluded by a heaven of cold stars, or an inferno of billowing gases. Further, it is estimated that, in the constitution of matter, there is a tiny asymmetrical ratio of particle and anti-particle. If, for example, every proton had been perfectly matched by an anti-proton, there would have resulted a kind of mutual cancellation. But there is a minute excess breaking the symmetry, computed in

---

19. For a more philosophical approach see John Jefferson Davis, 'The design argument, cosmic "fine tuning", and the anthropic principle', in *Philosophy of Religion* 22 (1987): 139–150.
20. Stephen Hawking, *A Brief History of Time. From the Big Bang to Black Holes* (New York: Bantam Press, 1988).
21. Hawking, *A Brief History of Time*, 121–123.
22. For some further explanation of these four forces and the efforts to bring them together in a 'Grand Unified Theory', see Ian G Barbour, *Religion in an Age of Science* (London: SCM Press, 1990), 126–8.

terms of one in a billion. It is this minute excess, this infinitesimal asymmetrical surplus, that becomes a window of opportunity for the emergence of the universe as we now know it.[23]

And here we are, in this moment of time, alive on this planet, immersed in this universe, just as the universe is alive to itself in our minds and hearts.[24] Our bodies, minds and hearts are part of an awakening cosmic mystery. Paul described the whole of creation as groaning in one great act of giving birth. He saw us human beings as groaning too, for the fulfilment that is not yet; more mysteriously, he understood the creative Spirit of God groaning within us to inspire hopes worthy of the mystery at work (Rom 8:18–28). In today's vision, the human is not alien to the earth, but embodied in its history and web of life. Nor is the earth an alien element in the universe, since it is the product of great cosmic forces at work in everything. It is all to be received as a gift—the gift of existence in a stupendous cosmic reality of unimaginable proportions and duration; the gift of life among other living things in this earthly biosphere; the gift of being consciously able to receive all this as a gift, and to turn to the Giver in ecstatic praise and thanksgiving.

In this sense of creation, we are all children of God, the Creator, and children of the universe, born of the earth. Though made in the image of God, and we are earthlings: we live only in a genetic solidarity with myriad other forms of life on this planet. If they serve and sustain us, we are called to a responsible stewardship of them. We human beings are related in a web of life with some millions of other species. Wombats and cassowaries, kookaburras and dolphins, frill-necked lizards and rainforest ferns, corals and all the teeming life of the reef– all connected in the one web of life, all relatives in this planetary coexistence. Elements of the stars are in the phosphorous of our bones. The same hydrogen which makes the stars burn, energises our bodies and powers our imagination.[25]

---

23. David Toolan, SJ, 'Nature as a Heraclitean Fire'. Reflections on Cosmology in an Ecological Age', *Studies in the Spirituality of the Jesuits* 23/5 (November 1991) [whole issue], 18–19.

24. For a fuller discussion of the Anthropic Principle', see Barbour, *Religion in an Age of Science*, 135–148.

25. For an accessible elaboration of this point, see Denis Edwards, *Made From Stardust*

In the words of Francis, Christians are also called on,

> . . . to accept the world as a sacrament of communion,
> as a way of sharing with God and our neighbours on
> a global scale. It is our humble conviction that the
> divine and the human meet in the slightest detail in the
> seamless garment of God's creation, in the last speck of
> dust of our planet [9].

Current perceptions of time and space, and of the evolutionary
dynamics and cosmic emergence as explored by science,
provoke a fresh posing of the age-old question of creation. From
one authoritative source, namely, John Paul II, we hear, 'If the
cosmologies of the ancient Near Eastern world could be purified
and assimilated into the first chapters of Genesis, might not
contemporary cosmology have something to offer to our reflections
upon creation?'.[26]

How, then, can the question of creation be posed in such a
startlingly different context? In addressing such a question it is of
great importance to base our thinking in as broad and inclusive
fashion as possible. Aquinas in a homily asserts,

> God, like a good teacher, has taken care to compose
> most excellent writings that we may be instructed in
> all perfection. 'All that is written', says the Apostle, 'is
> written for our instruction'. And these writings are in
> two books: the book of creation and the book of holy
> scriptures. In the former are so many creatures, so
> many excellent writings that deliver the truth without
> falsehood. Wherefore Aristotle, when asked whence it
> was that he had his admirable learning, replied, 'from
> things which do not know how to lie'.[27]

(Melbourne: Collins Dove, 1992).

26. From an address to the Vatican-sponsored seminar commemorating the three
    hundredth anniversary of Newton's *Philosophiae Naturae Principia Mathematica*, in
    Origins 18/23, (17 November 1988): 376.

27. Thomas Aquinas, *Sermo V, in Dom 2 de Adventu* (Vives XXIX), 194.

The value of scientific objectivity is evident in Thomas' confident intellectual commitment to 'the things that do not know how to lie'. The challenge today is re-appraise the seemingly simple requirement of being objective and to recognise where wonder at the mystery begins. It begins by realising that the activity of reflecting on creation is *human* reflection—the work of human minds. In both the past and in the present, the emphasis on objectivity, that is, on what is independently 'out there', is so great that human consciousness was regarded as one 'thing', as it were, in a world of other 'things'. It is easy to forget the inwardness of consciousness through which we are aware of reality and respond to it in wonder and questioning. Aquinas, early in his career wrote of the human soul as the most mysterious entity within creation and with its intimate relationship to the Creator: 'God is the greatest of all goods and more proper to each one than anything else can be because he is closer to the soul than the soul is to itself'.[28]

God cannot, therefore, ever be reduced to a patriarchal projection, nor to a temporary stop gap, nor to a particular cosmic force, and so forth. Rather, God is limitless intelligence and love that gives rise to the universe in which our knowing and responsive selves can operate. God is the Light in which the human mind participates, as it progressively illuminates what is, just as God is the love which we share as we grow in responsibility and concern for what should be.

Our conscious experiences of observing, imagining, understanding and valuing are dimensions of the actual universe.[29] These activities are the aspects of creation with which we are most familiar. They make the question of creation freshly and piercingly intimate. The character of the universe is felt in the ultimate attractiveness of the values of truth, goodness, justice, compassion. By including in our explorations the experience of our wondering, knowing, and responsible selves, we arrive at a sense of being beholden to the Other, the source, enablement and fulfilment of all our searching.

---

28. Thomas Aquinas, *III Sent*, d. 29, 1, 3, 3.
29. For an impressive survey, see Brendan Purcell, *From Big Bang to Big Mystery: Human Origins in the Light of Creation and Evolution* (New York: New City Press, 2015), especially 107–145, 320–334.

We find ourselves, not at the controlling centre of the universe, but as participating in its limitless mystery. We are caught up and carried along in a great cosmic unfolding, precisely as it presents us with ourselves in this actual world and as breathing the atmosphere of this planet. To us it has been given to participate in the universe, to live in this world, to celebrate its varied wonder, contribute to its direction in love, and yield to its promise in hope. We can come to an ecological awareness, as relationally located in the whole web of life and carried the wave of all that moves and sustains our existence, in body, mind and heart. The world shimmers with intelligibility in our minds, thrills with its goodness in our hearts, and bursts into our imagination with its beauty. At no point are we dispassionate observers, but always ecstatic participants in the wonder of existence and the great mystery of life.

The question of creation and its Creator are inscribed into the dynamics of our unfolding experience. What is the creativity that has sustained and moved the unfolding of the universe? Different levels of answers deal respectively with, say, molecular structure, biochemical organisation, evolutionary genus, social organisation and technological achievement. No doubt, one can spend a life-time devoted to any one of these. But at no point are we forbidden to pose the radical question: Why is there this something rather than nothing? If we are ecstatically immersed in a world of meaning, truth, value and beauty, what is the ultimate ground and goal of such ecstatic openness?

For Aquinas, God is more intimately present to each and every existent reality than it is to itself. He explains,

> God is present in all things, but not as part of their nature, nor as a modification of their being, but in the way something which acts is in contact with what it acts upon . . . Since God is by nature sheer Be-ing, it must be he who causes be-ing in creatures as his characteristic effect . . . God has this effect on created realities not only when they first begin to be, but as long as they are kept in being . . . Indeed, 'to-be' is that which is the most

intimate to each reality, and what most profoundly inheres in everything . . . God must be in everything, and in the most interior way.[30]

The 'to be' of the creature is more easily understood as a process of becoming, guided by the continuously creating Creator. In the words of Denis Edwards,

> Theology affirms that what enables the creature to be what it is, and enables it to become more than it is in itself, is the power of active self-transcendence, which is the pressure of the divine being acting upon creation from within . . . Evolutionary change is empowered by the dynamic presence of the absolute being of God. Evolutionary change occurs because of the presence of transforming love, which continually draws creation to a surprising and radically new future from within.[31]

Such a sense of God acting in creation places any understanding of evolution in a gracious context. As the encyclical states, 'The Spirit of God has filled the universe with possibilities and therefore, from the very heart of things, something new can always emerge' [51]. But if that evolutionary understanding slips out of a larger context of intelligibility, it gives the impression of having an all-mastering comprehension of the emergent reality of the world. We begin to persuade ourselves that we actually know where we have come from and where we are going. The past and the present are emptied of any significance save in terms of endless, perhaps aimless, further development. Nothing has value in itself. When a species dies out, and most do, its existence is not to be reduced simply to a failure in finding a place in an evolutionary future. Nor does the singular individual have significance only as a member of a species. A genuine sense of creation lives in an atmosphere of adoration, thanksgiving

---

30. *STh* I, q. 8, a. 1.
31. Edwards, *Jesus and the Cosmos*, 53–55. For a different context, see J Moltmann, *The Way of Jesus Christ* (London: SCM, 1990), 297–301.

and reverence. To exist is most radically to be, not from or for or with oneself alone, but to 'ex-ist', to be 'out of oneself'. It is to live ecstatically, centred in the originating mystery which moves and attracts the universe to its fulfilment.

God, therefore, is the cause operating in all causality and creativity, a *transcendent* cause, in philosophical language. Divine Be-ing is not a filler of gaps, but that original matrix in which 'we live and move and have our being' (Acts 17:28), to quote Paul (probably citing Epimedines), who is 'above all, through all, in all' (Eph 4: 6).

There are some noteworthy contrasts to be drawn between the 'Big-Bang' approach of modern cosmology and the mystery of creation, the latter leads to adoration while the former commends a plausible scientific hypothesis. Further, creation is about the totality of gracious mystery implied in every *now*; the Big Bang is about a mathematically computed *then*. Belief in creation locates us in the God-given genesis of the universe, while the Big Bang concerns the material genesis of a cosmos. Creation is about how everything depends on God while the Big Bang focuses on our common emergence from one cosmic origin. The story of Creation tells of how the eternal God acts in freedom and love to call this universe into existence. The Big Bang begins the story of the universe as a temporal, spatial, unfolding cosmic event. Creation is an abiding mystery while the Big Bang is about the solution of a cosmological problem. Creation conveys, finally, a poetic, holistic sense of how all being, intelligence, value and beauty derive from their abiding Source, while the Big Bang is an elegant mathematical formulation in the proto-language, of cosmic origins.

When the universe dawns within our minds and hearts as God's creation, then divine Be-ing is recognised as the matrix from which all being emerges, the mysterious field in which everything participates. A sense of creation breathes an atmosphere in which thinking is most fittingly 'thanking-thinking'. Existence can only be thought as a gift. There are *data*, 'the givens', to be considered; but more fundamentally, there is the *donum*, the gift.

Acknowledging the gifted character of existence engenders a mood of thinking that is not self-centred. No one can aspire to be a cosmic know-all. Thinking is more like clearing a space in the midst of an ever-larger mystery. It speaks words out of, and into, an original silence. Whatever clarification our reverent thinking has to offer is attained only in reverence for a limitless unknown, in a more complete surrender to what is Other. Hence, the first and last movement of thought is neither control nor analysis nor the solution of problems. First and last, thinking is *thanking*—gratitude growing from the roots of our being, and expanding in the light of wonder and ever fresh discovery. It is ever under the necessity of giving thanks to *Someone*, the Giver of the uncanny gift of existence. In the words of St Francis, 'Most High, all powerful and good Lord, all praise is yours, all glory, all honor, all blessing . . .'[32]

Conclusion

This chapter has briefly explored key issues such as the meaning of creation, the activity of the Creator, the great tradition of faith-inspired cosmology represented in Maximus Confessor and St Tomas Aquinas—with all this confronted with changing scientific perceptions of the world. Discussion of such topics will enrich our understanding of integral ecology, just as they point more deeply into that ever-renewable resource from which Christian faith can draw, given the planetary extent of non-renewable resources, harmful dependencies and a suffering environment.

---

32. From *The Canticle of the Creatures* << http:/www.custodia.org/default.asp?id=1454>>

3

The Incarnation and Integral Ecology

From whatever perspective, the incarnation is the singular event informing Christian identity: ' . . . in him the whole fullness of the deity dwells bodily' (Col 2:9). As a culminating event in God's love for the world, the incarnation has a transformative effect on Christian consciousness in communication of a distinctive sense of God, the self, creation and the world. In this respect, the following citation from the twelfth century Benedictine Abbot Rupert of Deutz is instructive.[1] First, Rupert introduces the embodied unity of all in Christ:

> To the one and only Son of God and Son of Man, as to their head, all the members of the body are joined, all those who are received into the faith of this mystery, in the fullness of this love. Thus, there is one single body; it is a single person, a single Christ, the head with the members, who rises up to heaven, crying out in its gratitude and showing to God the church of his glory, 'Here is bone of my bone, flesh of my flesh!' and making seen that he and her come together in a veritable unity of person, he says further, 'and the two will be one flesh'.

Second, this early medieval Benedictine writer directs our attention to the expanding, sacramental reality of the flesh of Christ:

---

1. Rupert of Deutz, *De divinis officiis* l.2, c. 11 (PL 170.43a–c) (my translation). This quotation concludes Henri de Lubac's *Corpus Mysticum: L'Eucharistie et l'église au moyen age ; Étude historique* (Paris: Aubier, 1948).

Yes, there is a great mystery. The flesh of Christ which, before the passion, was the flesh of the sole Word of God, has so expanded by the Passion, it is so increased, and it has so filled the universe that all the elect who were from the beginning of the world or will live to the last among them, by the action of this sacrament that makes of them a new dough, he brings together in one Church where God and man are eternally united.

Third, Rupert emphasises the paschal reality of Christ's transformed embodiment:

This flesh was only at first a grain of wheat, a single grain before it fell into the ground to die there. And behold now that it died, it increases on the altar, it bears fruit in our hands and in our bodies; and while the great and rich Lord of the harvest ascends, he takes up with him right to the barns of heaven this fruitful earth in the heart of which he has increased.

How an integral ecology incorporates such an incarnational and sacramental vision is the major concern of this theological reflection. How does the incarnation expand so that Christ 'takes with him . . . this fruitful earth in the heart of which he has increased.'

Pope Francis in a paragraph of *Laudato Si'* reminds his readers that 'The New Testament does not only tell us of the earthly Jesus and his tangible and loving relationship with the world. It also shows him risen and glorious, present throughout creation by his universal Lordship' [100]. Since 'the fullness of God' dwells in Christ, the crucified and risen One, he is the agent of reconciliation and peace (Col 1:19–20). Christian faith leads to the hope that at the end of time, 'the Son will deliver all things to the Father, so that 'God may be all in all' (1 Cor 15:28). In his promotion of an integral ecology, the Pope introduces a particular Christological perspective on the world of nature and the environment: 'The creatures of this world no longer appear to us under merely natural guise because the risen One is mysteriously holding them to himself and directing them towards fullness as their end' [100].

Clear points emerge of some relevance to an integral ecology:

1   Christian faith confesses Jesus Christ. It looks back to Jesus of Nazareth, a human being on this planet two thousand years ago, and now, it looks out in all directions to the risen One, present in all time and space;

2   Christ Jesus is the point of reconciliation, by his self-giving love, bringing together what was previously alienated and divided;

3   Christ is the focus of hope: he surrenders all creation to the Father, and though him, God brings to fulfilment of all that is;

4   Even now creation is being transformed in Christ as grace heals, perfects and transforms our world in view of its fulfilment in God.

But this theologically grand vision of the union of all things being transformed in Christ, has to contend with the complexity involved in being human. Our first topic, therefore, concerns the human question.

1. The Human Question

An essential cultural task for a genuinely integral ecology is to provoke an uninhibited conversation on the topic of our shared humanity. The current revulsion against the flat, quantitative, purely economic description of society, so favoured in modern politics, demands a larger frame of reference. More deeply still, the increasing robotisation of human language is a cause of irritation, if not alarm. Terms such as stimulus and response, conditioning, input and output, turned on and switched off, being burned out or blowing fuses, magnetism and the right chemistry, being programmed or brain-washed or hardwired, developmental cycles or stages, projecting the right image, software and hardware, and so on, figure in a current vocabulary. There is the obvious danger of linguistically reducing the total range of consciousness to the model of the machine, the computer, the camera, and chemical, physical or electrical interaction, and so detaching it from the earthly environment in which it unfolds. A total explanation of human consciousness is ever elusive—as instanced in Richard Tallis' vigorous, informed debunking of the idea that neuroscience can offer a complete explanation of what makes us human in his book *Aping Mankind: Neuromania and Darwinitis, and the Misrepresentation of Humanity.*[2] His work is all the more persuasive since the author is both a materialist and an atheist!

There remains, however, a daunting complexity. Levels of living and non-living things exist below, and before, the dawn of human consciousness. Each level looks beyond itself to something more. Sub-atomic particles assemble themselves into the elements of the periodic table. Chemical elements come together into increasingly complex compounds as in the structure of enzymes and acids within the living cell. Cells come together in all the variety of plant and animal life. Cellular structures, in turn, are subsumed into the astonishing emergence of the brains of the human beings, just as they participate in the ecological biosphere in the food they eat, the air they breathe, the water they drink, the wine of their celebrations.[3]

The universe envisaged in traditional terms was inevitably limited to a worldview of a stable, hierarchical order of natures. But that way of looking at the world has changed. There are dimensions of time and space, and relationships between mass and energy that were previously unimaginable. The world of our present understanding is a process, unfolding through billions of years in increasing

---

2. Richard Tallis, *Aping Mankind: Neuromania and Darwinitis, and the Misrepresentation of Humanity* (Durham: Acumen, 2011).
3. See Arthur Peacocke, *God and the New Biology* (London: JM Dent and Sons, 1986), 120–127.

differentiation of physical, chemical and biological forms. There are successive levels of organisation, from the quantum behaviour of particles to the formation of increasingly complex molecules to the emergence of life, from the protozoa to the millions of species we can now classify. The path of emerging differentiation heads to the phenomenon of the human, and its consciousness of the universe as a vast interrelated whole.

The specific difference of the human is connected to the capacity to register meaning beyond sense impressions, to respond to value beyond instinctual attractions, and, with the progressive awakening of consciousness, to transcend the familiarity of a habitat with an ever-growing sense of a world and the universe in which we live. In that respect, there is a distinctiveness of the human which, however much it shares a genetic inheritance with other animals, must be respected—and defended. After all, there have been no reports so far of a pod of whales holding a conference on the declining quality of plankton; or of leopards gathering to plan a cosmetic makeover in order to change their spots; or of dolphins who, after meeting in prayer, have decided to assert the rights of fish. We have no information on lemmings exploring less wasteful organisational procedures, or of the higher apes writing monographs on the meaning of life. Any developments in such a direction have so far escaped detection. As a result, questions of meaning and value, of a universal sense of the totality and of our responsibility within it, seem to be left to the human.

Even though we *are* animal with the animals, it belongs only to the human among this planet's life-forms to experience the capacity for reflective intelligence and global responsibility. With all other animals, the human being breathes the air of this planet; but human consciousness inhales the atmosphere of another realm—that of spirit which exceeds the generative capacities of matter, and intimates the presence of ever-active, infinite source of intelligence and goodness.

From Aristotle on, previous generations spoke of the human as the 'rational animal' (*zoon logikon* in Greek, *animal rationale* in Latin). This was the classic description of the human as the biophysical life-form that can reflect on itself, and even reflect on its own reflecting, in an intelligence that is, in principle, open to everything. Evolutionary biology has taken as its particular focus the biophysical or 'animal' feature of human emergence. In this respect, we have new understanding of the process in which human existence has emerged. It amounts to a rediscovery of the basic animality of the human—so that it is not as though a human being is somehow circling the globe looking for a temporary physical habitation. The human animal shares with all other animals a common emergence and structure in a biophysical world, with needs, emotions, and the instincts to bond, reproduce, care for young and so forth.

Yet there remains the 'rational' aspect—that strange capacity in the human for thought and freedom. There is the capacity for reflective openness to everything—from the genetic makeup of our bodies and the brain's trillion neurons, to the phenomenon of consciousness itself—and all its manifestations in faith, science, philosophy, art. How, then, does the Incarnation fit into such a scheme? The paradox remains: the world is created in the Word; but that Word has entered the world, and dwelt amongst us in the 'flesh' of an evolving and unfolding cosmos. The Word, embodied in Jesus Christ, is personally and cosmically related to everything and everyone in the universe: the Incarnation, though singular, is not an isolated event.

Humanity is inevitably a question to itself.[4] The dynamics and structures implied in who we are and what we experience give rise to many distinctions: nature and person, male and female, body and soul, individual and the environment, society and culture, cosmos and history, God and the universe—these are just some of the dualities encountered by anyone disposed to look for answers— above all, in the domain of a truly integral ecology.

All this is far from a world of fixed and static natures whether these are imagined as more or less blended or juxtaposed. What

---

4.   For a classic treatment on the theme of the questioning character of human existence, see Eric Voegelin, *Order and History IV: The Ecumenic Age* (Baton Rouge: Louisiania State University Press, 1974), especially 316–330.

emerges is a kind of participatory interlinking of all levels of reality in the makeup of our humanity.[5] But a distinctively human consciousness has a universal range: indeed, from a cosmic point of view, the universe has become conscious of itself in the human body, mind and heart. As a result, the emergent and evolutionary dynamics of reality inevitably affect faith's understanding of the Incarnation.

Whatever the range of language and the variety of perspectives it provokes, the Incarnation is the necessarily focal meaning of the Christian understanding of this earthly humanity. In Christ, the world's path to God and God's way into the world are embodied: 'the Word became flesh and lived amongst us, and we have seen his glory' (Jn 1:14). Though the Word is uttered into the human history, it does not stop the human conversation, but provokes it to further questioning: '. . . what we will be has not yet been revealed' (1 Jn 3:2). In this respect, the first words of the Word in John's Gospel are instructive. They are in the form of a question: Jesus turns to the two disciples of the Baptist following him, to ask, 'What are you looking for?' (Jn 1:38). Indeed, we human beings and followers of Christ, in the midst of a planetary ecological crisis, are forced to hear this question anew: What, really, are we looking for in the light of Christ and this time in history?

2. The Word Incarnate in the World

If the incarnation is God's personal entry into human history, that event must involve participation in the cosmic process of emergence and evolution. The incarnation, therefore, suggests a divine affirmation of all the variety of factors involved in the genesis of life, humanity and the emergent world. In the world of God's creation and incarnation, nature possesses its own dynamism working in the complex interactions of atoms and molecules, DNA, cells, neurons,

---

5. See Rupert Sheldrake, *The Rebirth of Nature: The Greening of Science and God* (New York: Bantam Books, 1991), 100–108, for another, but associated vocabulary: *holons* as successively 'nested hierarchies'. At each level, the *holons* are wholes containing parts which are themselves wholes containing lower-level parts, and so on.

organs, organisms, bodies, bondings, populations, eco-systems and the biosphere of this planet. Because God's infinite creative Act is involved in each of these activities, because the creative process is initiated and finalized 'in Christ' (Col 1:15–20), a higher integration is entailed at each step in the process of emergence. Apart from that dynamic process, there could be no higher self-realisation than in the emergence of the human, and in human minds and hearts made open to the Word made flesh in this terrestrial milieu. Alert to the polarities inherent in any discussion of the human, the great saint of East and West, Maximus the Confessor, as we have already mentioned, speaks of the human being as 'the laboratory in which everything is concentrated and itself naturally mediates between the extremities of each division, having been drawn into everything in a good and fitting way through its development'.[6]

Clearly, a contemporary theology of the Incarnation must develop in a world immeasurably more vast, intricate, and disenchanted, compared to what previous generations could have imagined. As a result, the classic New Testament perspective of the prologue of John's Gospel, for instance, can be interpreted at a new depth and breadth, given its sense of the universe of God's creation centred in the Word made flesh.[7]

> In the beginning was the Word, and the Word was with God, and the Word was God. He was in the beginning with God. All things came into being through him, and without him not one thing came into being (Jn 1:1–3).

For John, the divine *Logos* is all-creative and inclusive: 'all things' came into existence through him, and depend on him, in some

6. Maximus Confessor, *Difficulty* 41:1305B. See Andrew Louth, *Maximus the Confessor* (London: Routledge, 1996), 19–33. I follow Louth's translation. See also, Lars Thunberg, *Man and the Cosmos. The Vision of St Maximus The Confessor* (New York: St Vladimirs's Seminary Press, 1985), 132–137.

7. For a fuller theological consideration of the prologue, see John Macquarrie, *Jesus Christ in Modern Thought* (London: SCM, 1990), 105–122. Macquarrie's own translation of this passage, especially his use of 'meaning' for *Logos* is particularly imaginative. For a fuller discussion, see Anthony J Kelly and Francis F Moloney, *Experiencing God in the Gospel of John* (Mahwah, NJ: Paulist, 2003), 29–60.

causal sense, in their origins, just as all meaning and intelligibility derive from God's self-meaning in the *Logos*. The verses which follow suggest the quality of human consciousness as 'light' and 'life' derived from the Word:

> All things were made through him, and without him, nothing was made. What took place in him was life, and the life was the light of humankind. The light shines in darkness, and the darkness has not overcome it (Jn 1:3-5).

In the vocabulary of faith, the meaning of 'God' begins from, and returns to, this Word who is 'with God' in the beginning. Nonetheless, the Word is not an abstract principle, but 'he', *this one*, (Jn 1:3-4, 10-11). An actual addressable subject is implied, one whose original identity will unfold only in the conversational world of human subjects and in the environment in which they live. The people he meets, confronts and calls will know him as 'you', and all the ages of history refer to him as 'he', Jesus of Nazareth.

'All things came into being through him' (Jn 1:3a): despite the differences existing among all created things, and despite their difference, even in their alienation, from God, the *Logos* is the genetic and unifying principle of the universe. The diversity of creation is still a '*uni*-verse' because of its origin and coherence in the Word. All of creation is a field of divine communication, being 'Word-ed' into being. This is the fundamental 'logic' of the Gospel: nothing has meaning outside the divine *Logos*. Nothing and no one stands, in its own right, outside the primordial Word.[8]

The *Logos*, by reason of the incarnation and the mission of the Son, creates a *dia-logical* (and even *ecological)* space in which Jesus will enter into conversation with all the range of *dramatis personae* involved in the dramatic unfolding of the Gospel narrative. Addressed by this Word, they will evince acceptance, incomprehension, hesitation,

---

8.　*STh*, 1, 34, 3: 'Because God understands both himself and all things in one act, the single divine Word is expressive, not only of the Father, but also of all creatures.'

doubt, questioning or rejection, or any combination of such attitudes. The Word, dwelling amongst us (1:14b), thus opens a unique field of communication. Indeed, the 'God-ward' (*pros ton theon*) status of Word in the first verse of the prologue presumes a certain dialogical dimension within the divine mystery itself.

The extremes, on the one hand, of enclosing God and creation within the sameness of human experience, and, on the other, the sense of an unbridgeable gulf permitting no communication between God and the world, are met with what is always implicit in the Johannine vision. In the light of the incarnation, the ultimate meaning of God and the radical meaning of the universe—and of ourselves and our environment within it—are ultimately intelligible only in reference to the incarnate *Logos*. The knowledge of faith is, therefore, in the deepest sense, 'ana-*logical*', governed and proportioned in accord with the concrete singularity of the One who has chosen to share the flesh of this world and to live 'amongst us'.

Since *he* is the Word both of God, and of the universe of all that exists because of him, a new way of speaking about God is set in motion. The classic themes of Word, being, life and light common to all ancient philosophies and religions are subsumed into a new mode of meaning. God is not known by a further refinement or extension of notions inherent in human traditions. All such are given a new twist by being tied to the singular and the personal—'earthed', as it were, in the story of the man, Jesus Christ. Divine revelation entails an encounter with the Word made flesh, and with the story he tells and embodies. God is thus 'ana-*logically*' knowable as the One revealed in the expressiveness and resonance of this Word.

In contrast to an exclusive understanding of the Word as an englobing cosmic presence, the focus is shifted to an event within creation and its history. Where before all things came to be in the Word, now that Word comes to be within that universe.[9] The singular

---

9. For this interpretation of 1:3b-4, see FJ Moloney, *Belief in the Word: Reading John 1-4* (Minneapolis: Fortress Press, 1993), 30–34. For a magisterial overview of the Word's coming to be within the becoming and evolving universe, see Karl Rahner, 'Christology within an Evolutionary View of the Word', in *Theological Investigations* V, translated by Karl-H Kruger (Baltimore: Helicon, 1966), 157–192. Rahner's article can

advent of the Word as the source and form of true life has occurred. This life is evidenced in the new consciousness made possible by what has happened: 'and the life was the light of humankind' (Jn 1:4). The Word, therefore, throws light on who God is, on what the world of creation is, and on the promise inherent in human destiny.

We pass now to the expanding cosmic horizon in which the Word is made flesh.

3. The 'Body Language' of the New Testament

The Christian community lives the presence of Christ *performatively*, that is, through the mediations of liturgy and preaching, in its missionary outreach and dialogical encounters, in its serving Christ in the neighbor—and in the neighbourhood—and even loving the enemy. In this respect, the Church is the historically embodied mediation of Christ. As we shall see in chapter 5, its paradigmatic moment occurs in celebration of the Eucharist as the sensible, sacramental, and relational setting of the Body of Christ. Eighteen hundred years ago, Irenaeus of Lyons had to deal with Gnosticism, the heady 'new age' spirituality of his day. He laid down a basic rule for every age of the church: 'Our way of thinking is attuned to the Eucharist; and the Eucharist in turn confirms our way of thinking.'[10] Thus, the Eucharist is the basic criterion of incarnational sensibility and imagination. It is not simply a memorial intent on recapturing the past, nor an extrapolation of the present into an unknown future. It is rather an embodied instant, in which both past and future are brought into the intense relational realism within the living environment of our existence.

On the other hand, the Church is the Body of Christ in more than a metaphorical sense. There is special realism of the Church's

---

be read as a particularly effective transposition in an evolutionary world-view implied in Aquinas' words: 'The mission of divine person can be taken as implying, from one point of view, a procession of origin from the sender; and from another perspective, a new way of being in what is other. Thus the Son is said to be sent by the Father into the world, in that he begins to be in the world in the visibility of the flesh he has taken to himself.' (*Summa Theol*, 1, 43, 1)

10. Irenaeus, *Adv haereses* 4.18.5; PG 7.1.1028.

union with the crucified and Risen One whose body is the organ of God's communication in the world. In the words of Augustine,

> If, therefore, you want to understand the body of Christ, listen to the Apostle telling the faithful, 'but you are the body of Christ and its members' (1 Cor 12:27). So if you who are the body of Christ and its members, it is your own mystery that has been placed on the Lord's table; what you are receiving is your own mystery. You say *Amen* to what you are, and when you say that, you affirm what you are. You hear, 'the Body of Christ,' and you reply, 'Amen!' Be, then, a member of the body of Christ in order to make that *Amen* true. [11]

The Church, in this realist sense, is the 'live performance' of incarnational faith as it celebrates the Eucharist in the midst of creation and the given environment.[12] As the Eucharist forms the Church and the Church performs the Eucharist, a unique 'body language' is implied though this can hardly be appreciated if a reductively materialist understanding of the body is in possession. For the body is more than what someone 'has' in a transient way, that is, as a physical organism and a delimited object in time and space. The human phenomenon of the body implies a personal 'somebody' organically immersed in a field of communication and relationships

---

11. See Augustine, *Sermo* 272 ; PL 38.1247 ; my translation of
    Corpus ergo Christi si vis intellegere, Apostolum audi dicentem fidelibus: Vos autem estis corpus Christi, et membra. Si ergo vos estis corpus Christi et membra, mysterium vestrum in mensa Dominica positum est: mysterium vestrum accipitis. Ad id quod estis, Amen respondetis, et respondendo subscribitis. Audis enim, Corpus Christi; et respondes, Amen. Esto membrum corporis Christi, ut verum sit Amen.
    For a less literal translation, see Augustine, *Sermons (230–272B) on the Liturgical Seasons, The Works of Saint Augustine: A Translation for the 21st Century*, partt 3, volume 7, translated by Edmund Hill; edited by John E Rotelle (New York: New City, 1993) 300.
12. A valuable reference here is Kevin J Vanhoozer, *The Drama of Doctrine: A Canonical Linguistic Approach to Christian Theology* (Louisville: Westminster John Knox, 2005) with its emphasis on the performative character of Christian faith.

with others and in a particular environment. The experienced reality of being this 'somebody' throws light on the 'body language' in which Christian faith expresses a distinctively incarnate mentality.[13] At the very least, that would mean acknowledging that the incarnate Word has not been 'ex-carnated' by being raised and assumed into heaven. Though he is indeed 'out of sight' as far as the physical, historical presence among us of Jesus of Nazareth is concerned, he is not so lost in the clouds of heaven as to be removed from all human communication. The Incarnate One is not dematerialized into some other realm, so as to have no effect on the integral ecology we are exploring. It is, then, not as though he has become disembodied. Rather, it is better to confess that we human beings are not yet fully embodied in the Body of Christ. From this point of view, the resurrection-ascension of Christ is an expanding bodily event, in accord with God's continuing incarnational action in the world, involving ever more persons and ever more of the world as history unfolds.

An integral ecology does not call for the invention of some new form of celestial physics or super-terrestrial biology. No doubt, science will continue to astound us with its explorations. The humble contribution of theology, however, to an integral ecology arises from focusing on the phenomenon of the primal Christian event—the incarnation, and what this means for human identity and the way the world and its environment is to be understood and appreciated.

While a reflective faith must continue to build connections with philosophical and scientific world views, it cannot do so without a heightened receptivity to the distinctiveness of its own data. Before theology can be 'faith seeking understanding', its necessary first step is to be attentive, not only to what has been given to understand, but also to the way it has been given—as gift. From the experience of faith and of participating in this earthly environment, the mind

---

13. In the labour of *distinguer pour unir*, many distinctions need to be made that cannot be treated here—between body and soul, matter and spirit, person and community, the one and the many, the church and the world, etc; these are some of the distinctions necessary for a full exploration of what the Body of Christ means.

moves from the given to the gift, and to the source and goal of such giving.[14] There is much to be learned from the generalized phenomenology of revelation: what appears as the given, must be allowed to be registered on its own terms—that is, as a gift—before hurrying to press it into other frames of reference.[15] The phenomenality—or mode of givenness—of the total Christ event can be so blocked by a narrowly empiricist point of view that it tends to take body as something I 'have as *my* body', as one among innumerable physical bodies. Rather, the body or to be embodied is to participate in a field of intentionality. The focus is the manner in which an embodied consciousness is informed by relationships, actual or possible, to everything and everyone involved in one's life in this world—God, and the other—human, environmental and cosmic.[16] The human body is, of course, a physical and physiological object. It is both legitimate and indeed desirable that it be treated as such, and its unique complexity explored, as with the stupendous neural complexity of the human brain. But the consideration of *somebody* only in this way, detached from personal, interpersonal, environmental and universal consciousness, is to relegate it to an alien state.

But things appear differently when the body is appreciated as the 'saturated phenomenon' of a unique *somebody*. It is disclosed through a special sense of immediacy and unobjectifiable intimacy in regard to oneself and others. In this regard, we can distinguish the 'body-subject' from the 'body-object'.[17] The 'body-subject' is not merely something I possess, but is rather the field of my communication with the other, personal and transpersonal. This body intimately constitutes the subject's being *somebody* in the

---

14. See Anthony J Kelly, *The Resurrection Effect: Transforming Christian Life and Thought* (Maryknoll, NY: Orbis. 2008),15–23, 24–43.

15. Rolf Kühn, 'Phänomenologische Leibbegriff und christologische Inkarnation', in *Münchener Theologische Zeitschrift* 59 (2008): 239–55.

16. Anthony J Godzieba, 'Knowing Differently: Incarnation, Imagination, and the Body', in *Louvain Studies* 32 (2007): 361–382.

17. See Louis-Marie Chauvet, *Symbol and Sacrament: A Sacramental Reinterpretation of Christian Existence*, translated by Patrick Madigan, SJ, and Madeleine Beaumont (Collegeville, Minn: Liturgical, 1995), 146–55.

world. It implies possibilities of intimate self-giving and self-disclosure, as is eminently the case in erotic or maternal love. In this sense, the body-subject is the whole realm of incarnate consciousness, is a field of mutual indwelling, of being with, and for, the other, and of conscious interactions within a zone of incarnated relationships.[18] In the *eros* and generativity of love, one's bodily being is re-experienced in, with, through and for the 'flesh' of the other.[19] Thus, the body of my conscious being is affected by the encompassing phenomenon of the other and the world it embodies, and, in turn, affects it. It is at once an elemental bonding with the world, an immediate exposure to it, a multi-leveled participation in it, and a primal communication within it.[20]

By exploiting this notion bodiliness and this experience of embodiment, we begin to have an analogical sense of the bodily resurrection and ascension of Christ as inaugurating a new expansion of the incarnation and, consequently, a new way of relating to Christ. What the bodily dimension of this might entail, and what a connatural sensibility to it might mean, are dimensions of both being and consciousness that resist adequate expression. The dimensions of time and place as understood in former cosmologies and implicit in much of Christian tradition, are long surpassed. But that is not to say that they have been replaced by completely clear ideas. Even the meaning of energy and its various manifestations and material concretions are not areas of clear definition.[21] If this is the case, one is tempted to ask, would it not be better to bequeath

---

18. Jean-Luc Marion, *Le phénomène érotique: Six meditations* (Paris: Grasset, 2003), 170.

19. Marion, *Le phénomène* érotique, 185. John Paul II's treatment of this point is necessarily more general but still with a strong phenomenological emphasis. See John Paul II, *The Theology of the Body: Human Love in the Divine Plan*, foreword John S Grabowski (Boston: Pauline, 1997), 42–63.

20. Jean-Luc Marion, *In Excess: Studies of Saturated Phenomena*, translated by Robyn Horner and Vincent Barraud (New York: Fordham University, 2002) 100; *Le phénomène érotique*, 170, 180–81.

21. See *The Ghost in the Atom: A Discussion of the Mysteries of Quantum Physics*, edited by PCW Davies and JR Brown (New York: Cambridge University, 1993), 26. For further remarks, see James P Mackey, *The Scientist and the Theologian: On the Origins and Ends of Creation* (Dublin: Columba, 2007), 192–95.

the body exclusively to the explorations of science? Perhaps an integral ecology would be better advised to leave behind bodily and material concerns in order to concentrate on the spiritual self and its transcendence over matter. Though the incarnation is the original defining event, should not faith be now concentrated in, say, the gift of the Spirit in a less physical way?

Our point throughout this brief reflection, however, is that Christian theology—especially in its Christological and anthropological specializations—must continue its proper task as a dimension of integral ecology—which, in this instance, is to suggest the effect of the Incarnation on our sense of humanity and its world. An integral ecology must explore analogies with other notions of body—anthropological, phenomenological, scientific, aesthetic, etc.—that arise in other disciplines and styles of thought. In this respect, Christian body-language can call on a wide variety of analogies, old and new, to develop its meaning. In line with vision of Maximus the Confessor as referred to above, yet alert to the findings of modern cosmology, Teilhard de Chardin perceptively remarked,

> My own body is not these or those cells which belong exclusively to me. It is what, in these cells and in the rest of the world, feels my influence and reacts against me. *My* matter is not a *part* of the universe that I possess *totaliter*. It is the totality of the universe that I possess *partialiter*.[22]

With his christocentric perspective, Teilhard insists, 'Christ must be kept as large as creation and remains its Head. No matter how large we discover the world to be, the figure of Jesus, risen from the dead, must embrace it in its entirety.'[23]

---

22. Pierre Teilhard de Chardin, *Science and Christ*, translated by René Hague (London: Collins, 1965), 13.

23. Cited in Christopher Mooney, SJ, *Teilhard de Chardin and the Mystery of Christ* (London: Collins, 1966), 136. While I have been arguing for the unique realism of the Church as the Body of Christ, I am not thereby conceiving of the whole universe as his body, even though he is 'head', of all creation. I am leaving open the question of what that universal and cosmic headship entails.

Further, we cannot ignore the fact that today all are participants, however disoriented on occasion, in the amazing development of the 'cyberspace body' of our humanity. The pulse of electronic energies are extending not only our senses, but also our consciousness as body-subjects. The human body is in some measure being re-formed through the experience of new kinds of communication and a sense of 'being in contact' with others to a hitherto unimaginable degree. As writers such as Teilhard de Chardin and Walter Ong noted decades ago, such developments cannot be left unrelated to the event of the incarnation of the Word as it continues to expand throughout history.[24] Our understanding of the Word becoming flesh is extended not only to the evolutionary and ecological world, but also to the electronic or cyberspace dimensions of the world of communication.

We can ask, then, to what degree these developments contribute to our understanding of the expanding event of the Incarnation and the formation of the Body of Christ? If the spirit of human inventiveness and creativity has so transformed our embodied existence, how will the Holy Spirit, having already raised the Crucified One from the tomb and animated the Body of Christ, penetrate and transform all creation? In the present context, there are multiple relationships to be explored—between the Body of Christ, the humanity of the risen Lord, and the living reality of the Church celebrating the Eucharist as the sacrament of his Body and Blood, and in this terrestrial environment. The different aspects or realizations of Christ's Body are so interwoven, that one has a sense of a God-given corporeal field of incarnational communication, in contrast to the isolation of discrete entities.

---

24. See, for example, Walter J Ong, *Orality and Literacy: The Technologizing of the Word*, second edition (New York: Routledge, 2002).

Conclusion

The drift of our argument moves toward the one point, namely, the Incarnation as an expanding event in the economy of God's self-communication. It must affect the Christian sense of humanity, its world, and the universe overall. Christ is still the incarnate Word, and Christian self-understanding recognises that, to profess faith in Christ is to be members of his paschal Body. No uncritical univocity is implied such that would result in any kind of physical monophysitism or, more accurately, 'monosomatism', in understanding how the incarnate reality of Christ is related to this present bodily existence. Nor, on the other hand, is the Body of Christ reducible to a vague sense of a metaphorical or symbolic 'mystical body'. Something more vital, more material, more cosmic and specifically incarnational is involved. The rapid advances of science have led to a radically changed sense of matter, time, and space, and the cosmic interconnection of all things. The sensibilities of faith in the Word as incarnate in this material universe are affected. A problem arises when faith remains tethered to bypassed cosmological conceptions. To that degree, the Christian sense of the Body of Christ loses its assurance as a cosmic and historical reality, and veers toward a new kind of docetism. It is then defenceless against the soul-less body of materialistic modernity, and, for that matter, unable to deal with the bodiless soul of a rootless postmodernity.

When the life of faith is understood as an actual participation in the Body of Christ, there are realist consequences. There is in Catholic tradition a sense of intense physicality in the understanding of the real presence of Christ in the Eucharist. It must be admitted, however, that this does not always inspire a larger body-consciousness flowing from the Eucharist into every aspect of Christian life. This 'summit' and 'font'[25] of the life of the Church can, indeed, provoke ecological responsibility, an

---

25. Vatican II, The Constitution on the Sacred Liturgy *Sacrosanctum concilium* no. 10, http://www.vatican.va/archive/hist_councils/ii_vatican_council/documents/vat-ii_const_19631204_sacrosanctum-concilium_en.html (accessed July 26, 2010).

openness to the cosmic dimensions of faith, and inspire solidarity with the suffering, and, in the context of a nuptial mass, express a redemptive affirmation of sexuality. But to what degree do such developments of faith find their motivation in the incarnational action of God, ever in the process of forming the Body of Christ? It is almost as though the real presence of the Body of Christ, head and members, has been tabernacled in an interiority that has lost a sense of corporate and incarnate relationships. The reality of the one expansive Body of Christ slips out of the clear intentionality of faith. Of course, the doctrine of the incarnation continues to inspire a grand vision of human culture, but its assimilation is somewhat anorexic when it comes to bodily expressiveness in prayer, artistic imagination, community relations, moral conduct and care for the environment. While there is no need to fabricate some new ideology of body, there is need to recover a sense of participating in the Body of Christ in the cosmic and communitarian dimensions of the new creation. An extreme individualistic interiority works against the graced materiality and vitality of participation in the living Body of the Lord.

Many further questions need be faced if we are to appreciate the expanding character of the incarnation. It might be that a satisfactory answer will be beyond the epistemic capabilities and imagination of our age. There is no doubt that a full sense of the Body of Christ reserved to those most completely transformed into him. For the rest of us, it means remaining alert to the point of convergence of many aspects of faith: the risen Lord already fills the universe, and through the Eucharist forms the Body of the church as the dwelling place of God.[26]

Clearly, the incarnation is a doctrine of faith. But its reality is not only a cognitively objective datum. It inspires feelings and shapes sensibilities as it informs Christian consciousness, underpins

---

26. As Mary L Coloe, *Dwelling in the Household of God: Johannine Ecclesiology and Spirituality* (Collegeville, Minn: Liturgical, 2007), points out, it is not a matter merely of future existence in a divine realm, but also of God dwelling with us in the world, in the great household of faith (see also 1 Pt 3:21f; Acts 3:21).

relationships and inspires action. It is, therefore, constitutive of human identity and subjectivity. The Word made flesh affects the sense of the self and the depth and range of its participation in the world as 'our common home'.

4

Trinitarian Connections

The creed confesses God as Trinity in a communion of the three divine persons, Father, Son and Spirit. Any effort to relate the Christian sense of God to integral ecology cannot ignore the centrality of the Trinity. In the vision of faith, to be created is to be called into the divine love-life through the incarnation of the Word, through the outpouring of the Spirit—and, finally, to the face-to-face revelation of the Father. As *Laudato Si'* expresses it:

> The Father is the ultimate source of everything, the loving and self-communicating foundation of all that exists. The Son, his reflection, through whom all things were created, united himself to this earth when he was formed in the womb of Mary. The Spirit, infinite bond of love, is intimately present at the very heart of the universe, inspiring and bringing new pathways [238].

In this respect, the Trinity is presented, not so much in a doctrinal but in a contemplative mode.[1] Four points can be made:

1. The contemplation of faith extends from the presence of God in the world to the presence of the world in

---

1. Pope Francis is not alone in this. Apart from those he cites (Saints Bonaventure, Teresa of Avila, John of the Cross), the trinitarian testimony of William of St Thierry, Hildegard of Bingen, Meister Eckhart, Teresa of Avila, Elizabeth of the Trinity is a continuing resource. See Anne Hunt, *The Trinity: Insights from the Mystics* (Adelaide: ATF Press, 2010). The Conclusion (182–187) offers an especially valuable summary.

God. In that vision, the Trinity is the primordial source and circulation of the life of self-giving love. It draws creation into the movement of divine life and enables it to participate in the communion of the divine persons.

2. The Father, the first divine person, is the source of life within the Trinity itself, and the inexhaustible fount of love and mercy for the world.

3. Created in the Word, and claimed by the Word as his own through the incarnation, this Word and Son, the second person of the Trinity, is made flesh. This is to say that God personally enters this human habitat and environment, to be in every way a member of the human race.

4. Everything that lives and breathes is moved by the indwelling Spirit at work in the very heart of the universe to bring peace and reconciliation to the world, and to form the whole Body of Christ to the praise of the Father.

1. An Unusual Connection?

It is unusual to connect the environmental concerns of an ecological outlook to the sublime doctrine of the Trinity.[2] Earthly concerns, now so dramatically urgent, cannot be expected to recognize the relevance of what must appear as a remote and esoteric confession of three persons and one divine nature. Nonetheless, with the aim of developing an integral ecology, this encyclical makes a fertile connection, between care for our earthly home and the trinitarian life of God. In this case, it is not as though the terrestrial

---

2. There are exceptions: see the following, with their accompanying bibliographies, Denis Edwards, *Jesus, the Wisdom of God: An Ecological Theology* (Maryknoll, NY: Orbis Publications,1995); Anne Hunt, *Trinity: Nexus of the Mysteries of Christian Faith* (Collegeville, MN: Liturgical Press, 2005). See especially, chapter 5, 'Trinity and Creation, Ecology and Evolution', 94–116.

environment is being forced into an alien shape by imposing on it the highly wrought trinitarian doctrine hammered out in the early centuries of the Church for the purposes of orthodoxy. Rather, the aim here is to suggest the trinitarian dimension of all creation and the manner in which it connected within the one divine creative mystery, so to energise a profound appreciation of our common terrestrial home—as in the above cited words of *Laudato Si'*.

If Socrates declared 'the unexamined life is not worth living',[3] life, in Christian terms, is both examined and summoned to its highest reach, namely, as communion with the Father and the Son: '... that they may be one even as we are one, I in them and you in me, that they may be perfectly one ...' (Jn 17:22).

2. A Biblical Perspective

There can be no suggestion, therefore, that union with the One God means intimacy with infinite solitude. The One God does not live in self-contained isolation, but in the vitality of communion of interpersonal love and self-giving. The life of God, Father, Son and Holy Spirit, is communication and endless self-giving to the other. God is one, but in a unity-in-communion. Furthermore, the divine communion enfolds creation into itself—that we human beings may dwell in God and find our unity within the divine life. The words of Jesus in the Gospel of John are a focal reference—and of deep relevance to reflection on 'our common home':

> The glory that you have given me I have given them so
> that they may be one, as we are one, I in them and you
> in me, that they may be completely one (Jn 17:22)

A trinitarian understanding of God has its roots deep in the New Testament. Even the earliest letter, 1 Thessalonians (AD 51?) speaks in a straightforward uncomplicated manner about the threefold character of God (1 Thes 1:1–5). It is assumed that early readers

---

3.   See Plato, *Apology*, 38A.

will understand what is meant in such expressions.[4] A number of creedal and liturgical formulations are even more explicit as in the conclusion of Matthew's gospel, the Risen Lord commissions the disciples to go forth and baptize the nations 'in the name of the Father and of the Son and of the Holy Spirit' (Mat 28:19). In all such instances, there seems to be a settled liturgical usage, the most well-known being 2 Corinthians 13:14.[5]

For its part, John's Gospel attempts something more systematic, no doubt, influenced by the problems that inevitably arose because of the 'threefold' designation customary in early Christian communication. A significant aspect of John's presentation is its expression of the communion existing between the Father and the Son. To this degree, it points to a dialogue or conversation going on between them. The Word made flesh lives, we might say, a dialogical existence: his origin is from the Father, his identity is to be this Father's Son, just as his mission is to do the Father's will. Existing from and for the Father, he is sent from the Father, receives everything from him, yet is one with him. Still, 'the Father is greater than I' (Jn 14:28), for he is the origin and goal of all that Jesus is. No one goes to the Father but by him, but no one can come to Jesus unless drawn by the Father (Jn 6:44). The prayer of Jesus in John 17 is the climax of this kind of expression: 'that they may be all be one even as you, Father, are in me and I in you, that they also may be in us' (Jn 17:21).

The distinctive experience of the Church, that is, of those baptised in the name of the Father, Son and Holy Spirit, arises out of the singular

---

4. This manner of speaking is found, for example, in Paul's discussion of the law (Gal 3:11–14) and Christian freedom (Gal 4:4-6), just as it pervades his expressions of thanksgiving (2 Thess 2:13; Col 1:3-8), shape of his prayers (Rom 15:30; Phil 3:3-6; Eph 3:14–16) and conviction as to the unity and manifold grace of the Christian community (1 Cor 12:4–8).

5. Moreover, there is a kind of iconic element in the way the God is presented in a trinitarian form. See, for instance, in the Synoptics such as the various depictions of the baptism of Jesus: the Spirit descends in the form of a dove, the heavens are opened, the divine voice proclaims Jesus as the beloved Son (*cf* Mat 3:16–18; Mk 1:9–11; Lk 3:21–23; and also John 1:32–34); the Infancy Narrative (especially Luke) gives something like a holographic impression of God's saving presence: the Holy Spirit is the divine power at work, Jesus is uniquely the Son of the Most High (Lk 1:32–35).

mystery of divine self-communication. In this gift, a transparent reciprocity of relationships between the Father and the Son is implied. The Son is constituted, as it were, in his identity and mission through his relationship to the Father. For his part, the Father is constituted in his paternal self-giving in relationship to the Son. In every aspect of the being and action of the Word, there is the act of the Father's timeless self-utterance and engendering. The 'subsistent relationship' of the Father is revealed in sending his Son into the world, even while the identity of the Son is intelligible only as ceaselessly coming forth from the Father, the source of life and light.

And yet, there is the further coming of the Spirit. This is a gift of overwhelmingly positive significance for the disciples and Jesus himself. First of all, the Spirit of truth will guide the disciples into 'all truth' (Jn16:13). Secondly, as the Spirit of *truth*, he will glorify Jesus, taking what is his to declare it to the disciples (Jn 16:13) and showing that 'all that the Father has' is to be found in Jesus (Jn 16:15). In the light of these actions, the Spirit is, so to speak, a luminous and active presence in the history of faith. Through the witness of the Spirit, believers can penetrate ever more deeply into what has been going on between the Father and the Son. Post-biblical doctrinal developments will speak of the Spirit also as a 'subsisting relationship' between the Father and the Son.[6] Already at this stage of faith's expression, the Spirit is identified as 'in-between-ness' which makes possible for believers an entry into communion with God and into the fully bounty of the divine gifts. In this respect, the Spirit is the God-given manifestation of what the Father has communicated to the Son and, through him, to the disciples.

The Spirit comes, not to replace the message and mission of Jesus, but to make it a living reality in the history that is to unfold. In this sense, the Spirit is the light in which the opened heaven will be seen in all its truth (Jn 1:51). With the coming of the Spirit, time is no longer a pointless succession of instants, nor a continuing cycle of repetition. Rather time is now experienced as moving to a divine

---

6.   For a thorough survey and comment, see Gary D Badcock, *Light of Truth and Fire of Love*, 35–82; 145–170.

fulfilment when the Spirit comes to declare what is to come (Jn 16:13). There is a dynamism inscribed in time that looks to the full evidence of what God is bringing about. Jesus and the Father will come to make their home with those who, despite the conflicts that history will produce, have followed the path of faith (Jn 14:23). With the gift of the Spirit released through the death and glorification of Jesus (Jn 7:39), the community of faith will move to meet the Father 'in spirit and truth' (Jn 4:23–24). Consequently, the Father is not hidden, as one unknown, behind the mask of the Son. Rather, under the guidance of the Spirit, the community of faith finds in Jesus the true face of the Father turned lovingly toward it.

In terms of a biblical background, a Johannine perspective manifests the divine Three are a unity which is at once a communion of life, and a community of inter-related persons. In all that happens, the one God of Israel is at work, but with the singularity of a unique form of interrelationship as it is lived out between the Son and the Father. Clearly, this contrasts with any tendency to presuppose that the unity of the one God meant that God is ultimately alone, in effect, the absolute solitary.

A full hearing of the Word, however, depends on the gift of the Spirit. For this 'other Paraclete', 'the Spirit of Truth', whom the Risen Jesus sends, 'will teach you all things, and bring to mind all that I have said to you' (Jn 14:26). The Paraclete guides successive generations of believers into all truth (Jn 16:13), inspiring in them an understanding of Christ and guiding its development, even to this point of an ecological conversion in our day. A deeper and broader understanding of 'our common home' flows from the full realisation of what it means for the Word made flesh on this earth and in this world, and in this now threatened environment.

3. A Trinitarian Horizon

The contemplation of the Trinity inspires a deeper and broader ecological spirituality. Pope Francis considers the relational character of the divine persons and of the creation deriving from them. He writes:

> The divine Persons are subsistent relations, and the world, created according to the divine model, is a web of relationships. Creatures tend towards God, and in turn it is proper to every living being to tend towards other things, so that throughout the universe we can find any number of constant and secretly interwoven relationships [240].

Given its trinitarian origin and form, the universe of particular beings participates in the self-giving, self-expressive life of God. Creation is a network of relationships. Like the divine persons, the universe, and everything and everyone within it, is *from* and *for* the other. Made in the divine image and bearing the trinitarian imprint, all life is other-centred, and finds its origin, nourishment and completion in relation to the other.

Unfortunately, doctrinal controversies have often reduced this most illuminating and life-giving of Christian mysteries practically to the point of absurdity—at least in the minds of many Christians. What should have been the contemplation and celebration of God as the self-giving love at work in all things, and as the divine community enfolding all creation into itself, has been reduced to an exercise in supercelestial mathematics in which one could neither be multiplied, nor divided, by three. On the other hand, in recent years, trinitarian theology has been undergoing considerable renewal, so that a distinctively Christian vision and moral practice is informed by a trinitarian faith, and the theological perspective is sharpened.

First of all, God, as the one ultimate reality, is revealed as relational. In John's Gospel, for instance, the transparent reciprocity of relationships between the Father and the Son realign our understanding of the eternal reality of God, and the relatedness of God to the world in time. The Son is constituted, as it were, in his identity and mission through his relationship to the Father. For his part, the Father is constituted in his paternal self-giving in relationship to the Son. In every aspect of the being and action of the Word, there is the eternal act of the Father's timeless self-utterance and engendering. This is to say that the 'subsistent relationship' of the Father is revealed in his ceaseless generation of the Son, even while the identity and mission of the Son in intelligible only in his continuing coming forth from the Father, in order to reveal the primordial source of life and light.

The experience of God radically destabilises ordinary identities and relationships. God can no longer be 'kept in his place', for the Father has sent his Son into the world. For its part, the world itself has lost its self-made boundaries with what the Gospel of John calls the 'opened heaven' (Jn 1:51). Nor can Jesus be kept in his place, as he leaves this world to return to the Father. Even death ceases to be in place for him as an opaque impenetrable limit to human life. His dying is integral to the radiance of the love of God revealed in the self-giving of the Son. As for his disciples, though they will suffer the grief of their master's absence, his love 'to the end' (Jn 13:1) demands of them the mutual love that will leave them far more disturbed than any grief over his departure can cause. The reality of Jesus' absence leaves a space where no believer can ever live again in self-contained isolation: 'Just as I have loved you, you also should love one another' (Jn 13:34).

This interpersonal reciprocity and the mutuality of relationships described in John's Gospel led in the centuries ahead to the full blown Athanasian trinitarianism of the post-Nicene doctrine.[7] A seismic displacement of meaning occurred. Heaven has been opened (Jn 1:51). The truth of God's love occurs as an upheaval in the previously imagined world. The varied responses, of incomprehension, acceptance or scandalized rejection, make the words of the poet Paul Celan especially apposite: 'A RUMBLING: truth/ itself has appeared/ among humankind/ in the very thick of their/ flurrying metaphors.'[8]

---

7. For an excellent account of the theological development involved, see TF Torrance, *The Trinitarian Faith: The Evangelical Theology of the Ancient Catholic Faith* (London: T&T Clark 2000) , 47–75.

8. Paul Celan, *Poems*, translated by M Hamburger (Manchester: Carcanet, 1980) 202–203. (EIN DRÖHNEN: es ist/ die Wahrheit selbst/ unter die Menschen/ getreten,/ mitten ins/ Metapherngestöber.

What kind of reality is Christian faith trying to objectify out of its experience of God? How does such an experience affect the Christian's sense of reality—as in the present discussion of a genuine integral ecology? The imagination of trinitarian faith envisages ultimate reality as intrinsically relational. Theology, in order to avoid implying that the divine persons are three different substances, speaks of the divine persons as 'subsisting relationships'. That is to say, that the divine three are understood only in relation to one another, as *for* and *in* the other. Thus, the absolute one-ness of Father, Son and Holy Spirit is concretely realised in a pure self-communication to the other. God is God by being a communion of mutual self-giving. The very reality of God is, therefore, a communion of self-giving and other-directed love.

God as Father expresses his fullness in the Word, and accompanies such infinite self-expression with the act of infinite self-giving, in the love of the Spirit. In that self-utterance and self-gift, all that God is, all that the universe is or will be, all that the world is in its differentiated levels of life and existence, is contained. The universe, emerging in the long ages of time, is ever being called into existence by the gift of God. Consequently, the eternal *now* of trinitarian life is the matrix of time, not its contradiction.[9]

The relational vitality occurring within the eternal depth of God is named in theology as the 'divine processions' of the Word and the Spirit, creating the universe in its dynamic image. From the divine processions within God flows the 'process' of the universe unfolding through the ages.[10] This is to say that the divine processions are imaged forth in the unfolding of the cosmic process. The universe finds its ultimate coherence as the *uni-verse* in as much as the

---

9. For a rigorous examination of the theme of divine eternity, see John C Yates, *The Timelessness of God* (Lanham, Md: University Press of America, 1990).

10. I do not think this distinction is sufficiently appreciated. When it is not, 'process' becomes the ultimate reality, but not 'procession' in the trinitarian sense. There is a big difference between deifying the process and adoring the 'proceeding' divine persons. Even a survey of such towering expertise as Ian Barbour, *Religion in an Age of Science,* does not mention the relevance of the trinitarian mystery to current evolutionary and genetic understandings of reality. Remaining only with the category of process strikes me as being theologically far too timid.

Trinity draws all creation to participate in the relational life of God. Creation unfolds in the light of the Word, and is energised by the power of the Spirit, just as it lives in every moment in thankfulness to the originating love of the Father. From its experience of this relational field of divine presence, Christian faith comes to confess the Trinity as the transcendent presence immanent in the universe. All instances of being, becoming and life have their beginning, form and goal in the 'love-life of God so that God might be all in all' (1 Cor 15:28). The evocative language of Nicholas of Cusa returns such intense theological expressions to the world of mystical imagination: 'The Godhead is the enfolding and unfolding of everything that is. The Godhead is in all things in such a way that all things are in God.'[11]

The utterance of the Word 'in the beginning' (Jn 1:1) is the primordial self-expression of the Father. Through this communication, God is self-differentiated, the 'I' and the 'Thou', the 'I' and the 'We', the self and the Other. The universe, created in the Word (*Logos*) is a world of endlessly differentiated 'words' (*logoi*) or meanings. As Aquinas reminds us, 'created things cannot attain to the perfect image of God in a single form'. It was fitting 'that there be a multiplicity and variety in created things so that God's image be found in them perfectly in accord with their mode of being'.[12]

In the order of the Creed, the third divine person is breathed forth by Father and Son. The Love that differentiated itself as Father and expressed itself in the Son and Word, becomes, in the circulation of trinitarian life, the shared ecstasy of other-directed loving. The relational dynamics inscribed in the universe can therefore be understood as a participation in the unifying ecstasy of the Spirit. The Breath of God moves the differentiated, distinct, and independent realities of creation into self-transcending communion of the self with the Other. In this perspective, the cosmos lives

---

11. Quoted in Rupert Sheldrake, *The Rebirth of Nature: The Greening of Science and God* (New York: Bantam Books, 1991), 198. Noteworthy, too, is the influence of Sheldrake on the deep trinitarian structure of Bede Griffith's, *A New Vision of Reality*.
12. Aquinas, *Summa contra Gentes*, l. 2, c. 45.

and breathes the mystery of the original, expressive and unitive mystery of love at the heart of its existence.[13] If the original and ultimate reality is inherently relational, if ultimate unity is self-giving communion, trinitarian faith is a healthy disturbance of all closed little worlds of isolated independence. Defensive alienation from the other, resistance to peace and reconciliation, all deliberate disharmony or exploitation in regard to the rest of creation, set us outside the trinitarian flow of life.

3. Trinity and the World

A trinitarian conception of ultimate reality stands in contrast to a mechanistic worldview, however dominant and long entrenched. A mechanistically-modelled science has little patience with any theological vision, let alone one needlessly complicated with trinitarian references to processions, relationships, and the plurality of the divine persons. Nonetheless, current views of the processive and relational character of the cosmos might well find some aspects of trinitarian theology quite intriguing. Contemporary paradigms of science and some aspects of trinitarian thinking show signs of convergence, especially in a full-blown or integral ecology. After all, for two thousand years, trinitarian theology has come to regard ultimate reality as a realm in which occurs an eternal circulation of interpersonal, relational life in the fullness of truth and love. Such an understanding depends on a notion of God as concretely one only in a manifold of relationships. As a more holistic science becomes aware of this trinitarian perspective, dialogue is enabled, and a collaborative exploration of what constitutes ultimate reality is set in motion.

Traditional trinitarian theology after Aquinas passes from the consideration of the processions and relationships of the divine persons *ad intra* (that is, in the eternal 'within' of God) to their presence and relationships *ad extra*, in the God-created universe.

---

13. Here I have adapted three terms taken from John Macquarrie, *Principles of Christian Theology* (London: SCM Press, London, 1977), 195–202.

The self-communication of the Trinity to the created world, is treated under the heading of the biblical category of 'mission' or 'sending'— the way, for instance, God 'sends' the Son and Spirit into the world.[14] The processions of Word and Spirit within God are, as it were, prolonged into the world of time. Given the present evolutionary horizon, much can be gained by retrieving some aspects of the classic Trinitarian tradition.[15] We will now take some liberty with traditional terminology in the hope of making it more meaningful in the present context. For example, Aquinas asks, how can a divine person be 'sent'? The problem here is to imply neither inequality in the co-equal Trinity, nor a primitive form of spatial movement from one place to another, as though God were not everywhere in the first place. In answer to this question, Aquinas makes two points: First, The divine person is sent inasmuch as the eternal procession of the Son/Spirit is prolonged into time and history. In this, the divine consciousness takes in the world of time and its emerging world. Because the mission is an extension into time of the eternal procession, it means that the divine persons begin to exist in the world in a new way: 'Thus, the Son is said to have been sent by the Father into the world, even though he was already in the world, but now he begins to be in the world in a visible, incarnate way. The Word was made flesh.'[16] We can, therefore, understand the divine missions as the self-immersion of the Trinity in the created universe. The risk and the fragility, along with the beauty and dynamics of a temporal world, have been given a place in God's own trinitarian consciousness. In this way, the world is an aspect of God's own experience. From this point of view, the missions of Word and Spirit are the Trinity's opening out to the world in order to enfold creation into its communal life.

But there is a second point. Aquinas allows for two dimensions of divine communication, the 'invisible' and the 'visible' missions.

---

14. 14. For a creative treatment of the divine missions, see Robert M Doran, *The Trinity in History: A Theology of the Divine Missions* (Toronto: University of Toronto Press, 2012).

15. For an overview of Aquinas' approach to theology, see Anthony J Kelly, 'A Multidimensional Disclosure: Aquinas' Theological Intentionality', in *The Thomist* 67/3 (July 2003): 335–374.

16. *STh* I, q. 43, a. 1.

This traditional distinction, when properly understood, can prevent Christianity from being locked into a narrowness that would be ill-prepared for the cosmic scope of present challenge and responsibilities. For instance, in both the ecological integrity of our common home, and in interfaith dialogue, the Father's 'sending' of his Son and Spirit is deeply relevant.

So, first, a word on the *invisible missions*. We begin with the recognition that God is present to everything and everyone in an absolutely fundamental manner, as sheer Be-ing, *Ipsum Esse*, the source of all that is. It follows that, as the source of all being, God is present in the innermost depths of all reality. But from the depths of the ocean of Be-ing in which all exist, there comes a wave of divine freedom, of self-communicating love. God is not content, as it were, simply to be the nameless universal mystery at the heart of reality. Beyond giving us existence, the Trinity wishes to give itself to us in person, so that we can enter a new realm of selfhood and communion. This is the realm of grace. By receiving this new gift, we are not only God's creatures but also become God's intimates. The Trinity is recognised as acting through all creation in the vulnerability, creativity and unifying power of love.

The trinitarian self-communication brings about a transformation of human consciousness—traditionally called 'sanctifying grace'. Through this gift, a special intimacy with the divine mystery occurs.[17] The human self is 'conformed to God'. Through the experience of loving and being loved, the human person participates in the Spirit of love. Likewise, through the gift of faith and wisdom, believers share in the light of the Word: 'because by such knowing and loving, created consciousness (*rationalis creatura*) lives actively in contact with God. The special mode of the interaction involved means not only that God is intimately present to human consciousness, but also dwells within us as in his temple.'[18] The horizon of God's

---

17. *STh* 1, q. 43, a. 5, ad 2.
18. Thomas also speaks of the Father as given and indwelling through grace, but not as 'sent' (see *STh* I, q. 43, a. 3. The first divine person is present precisely as the source of all divine life and love, the Father who is 'above all and through all and in all' (Eph 4:6).

loving presence includes all time and space, for the Word and Spirit are said to be 'invisibly' sent to the human heart and mind. However unnamed and inexpressible this gift might be, the depths of human consciousness are stirred, and lifted to a new level of life and communion with God. The human being, however implicitly, begins to participate in the very consciousness of God's own knowledge and love. Wherever there is evidence of a consciousness lovingly alive, in reconciling wisdom and self-transcending love, it is evidence of the indwelling of God, a manifestation of the 'state of grace'. The Word of God is not some abstract form of information, but is given so as to reach the heart: 'for the Word is not any kind of word, but the Word breathing love.'[19]

The metaphor of 'mission' might give the impression of the divine Word and Spirit being sent from some kind of outer space where God dwells. On the other hand, once the spatial limits of the metaphor are recognised, the reality of the divine missions is more like an emergence of the mystery out of the depths of existence where God is ever present. What could have appeared to be a universe of simple fact, however uncanny, now appears as a radiant field of communication. God dwells in us and we dwell in God in the circulation of divine life and love.

But there is more. The divine missions are not only 'invisible' in that the Word and Spirit illuminate and enkindle human consciousness within the indefinable horizon of life. There are also *visible* missions. The divine Word who had been invisibly present in grace, becomes incarnate, in time and space, and in a particular terrestrial environment. The Spirit, too, who had invisibly dwelt in the hearts of all good people, is manifested in an historical event. The promised coming of the Spirit transforms lives and forms communities of faith, hope and love. The gift of the Spirit is an energy revealed in many gifts, and animates the whole life and ministry of the Church. Because the reality of God's self-giving is attuned to the embodied reality of our human existence, there is a visible dimension. God's self-communication takes shape, therefore, in the time and space of this particular world. God is not to be found

19. *STh* I, q. 43, a. 5, ad 2.

only in a transcendent spiritual realm, but more so in the flesh-and-blood of our world. Aquinas remarks,

> Now it is connatural for a human being to be guided by the visible to the invisible. Through the evidence of creatures, God has in some way manifested himself and the eternal processions of the persons. Likewise, it is right that the invisible missions of the divine persons be made manifest through visible creation. Now this occurs in one way with the Son, and in another way with the Holy Spirit: . . . the Son is visibly sent as the author of holiness; but the Spirit as the witness to that holiness.[20]

The embodied world of our existence is the natural milieu for human communication. Trinitarian communication respects this given 'ecology' of human existence in order to draw human beings into the divine life of communion. The created world, in all its differentiation, structures, relationships, and dynamics already manifests the relational and communicative reality of God. Although a trinitarian dynamism is originally inscribed into every element of the created world, this trinitarian orientation of creation is further intensified. The visible mission of the Word incarnate in Jesus Christ expresses in the world of human communication the transcendent mystery of God at work. And the Spirit, symbolised in the water, the wind, the air, the flame of our natural experience, opens into the field of ultimate connections. In the words of Francis:

> This leads us not only to marvel at the manifold connections but also to discover a key to our own fulfilment. The human person grows more, matures more and is sanctified more to the extent that he or she enters into relationships, going out from themselves to live in communion with God, with others and with

---

20. *STh* I, q. 43, a. 1. For further treatment of the missions, Jean-Hervé Nicolas, OP, *Synthèse dogmatique: de la Trinité à la Trinité* (Paris: Beauchesne,1985), 231–265.

all creatures. In this way, they make their own that trinitarian dynamism which God imprinted in them when they were created. Everything is interconnected, and this invites us to develop a spirituality of that global solidarity which flows from the mystery of the Trinity [240].

Three points bear stressing:

1. Since our being is fundamentally relational, the fulfilment of such relational existence consists in living out our manifold relationships to the Other, namely to God, to our neighbor, and to the neighborhood of 'our common home'. The implication is that, if any of these levels of relationship is denied, existence is distorted.

2. A deep sense of global solidarity flows from, participates in, and finds its ultimate fulfilment in, the mystery of the Trinity.

3. A contemplative awareness of the trinitarian dimension of this relational universe gives rise to a spirituality of relationships. A consciousness transformed in the love of the Spirit, in the light of the Word in whom all things were made, and in adoration of the Father who will be all in all, brings the gift of new vision. The world can be contemplated as indwelt in its every fiber by the Trinity just as that finite world dwells in God to receive a continuous outpouring of divine love and wisdom.

4. An Expanding Spirituality

A spiritual sense of reality is urgently needed when the present historical phase of rapid globalisation and the planetary proportions of our human co-existence are being brought together. A universal notion of human nature is now earthed in the actuality of a common human history. The peculiar crisis of our times turns on the question of how particular histories and cultures can meet for mutual enrichment in one planetary history. In this respect, the concern is not only for individual conscience struggling for authenticity, but also for the global conscience now being worked out in history under the pressure of a threatened environment. Any judgment on what is happening, however intimately personal it may be, cannot ignore the evidence that can only emerge through research and collaboration on a global scale. Individual and collective efforts occur in the context of our existence on this earth, a planet of an average sized star in a galaxy in which a hundred billion stars are said to shine, in the immensity of a physical universe of millions of galaxies, within a cosmic history of nearly fifteen billion years. Against such a background, it is easier to see that personal and social values must be earthed in the ecological well-being of the planet itself: loving our neighbour cannot afford to neglect a love for the planetary proportions of the neighbourhood. And if this novel historical process of global humanisation is to succeed in the face of the biases toward individual and group selfishness, an enormous but self-transcending common effort is required to recognise the objectivity of values such as truth, justice, freedom and compassion. Without these, progress will be impossible, with results that are all too easily named.[21]

Human history has reached a limit from which there is no retreating from questions dealing with previously unexplored territory—the future of life on this planet, human destiny, and God. At this point, trinitarian faith begins to operate in a larger and ever more challenging context. The Trinity has not ceased being present and active at this time just because our view of the world has expanded and the times have become more critical. The God continues to give himself into the world as it is. The Father's love is the eschatological horizon summoning history forward to that house of many rooms (Jn 14:2), in anticipation of the end when God

---

21. For a fuller treatment of these aspects, see Anthony J Kelly CSsR, *An Expanding Theology: Faith in a World of Connections* (Sydney: EJ Dwyer, 1991), 1–68; 157–167.

will be all in all (1 Cor 15:28). In the worship of the Father, all local and cultural situations are relativised—'neither on this mountain nor in Jerusalem' (Jn 4:21)—as God seeks true worshippers 'in spirit and in truth' (v 24). The Father works to bring human history to its true freedom in a solidarity unrestricted by time, place or culture. The Father, the God who sends both the Son and the Spirit,[22] is to be revealed as fulfilment of human searching in a 'face to face' vision. In this sense, The Father's love is found both at the beginning of our history, and as its absolute fulfilment in the future. But hope has to contend with all forms of despair over the fate of the world, and even the possibility of environmental disintegration.

If human history is to live in an horizon of hope, it must enjoy confidence in intelligence, in the ability to understand, and to come to the truth. The search for truth is obviously threatened by a dispirited mentality of suspicion concerning our capacities to arrive at truth and to understand reality. Intellectual diffidence of this kind restricts knowledge to an instrumental function of manipulating data in view of some pragmatic outcome. Similarly, morality is reduced to being merely the ethics of utility and the rules of exchange. The ultimate question is never far below the surface: is there is any meaning in our efforts to make sense our world? Is there any *Logos* in all the '*-ologies*' of human culture, beyond technical calculations of good outcomes for the job in hand? An integral ecology, in contrast, demands the intellectual integrity that comes from a dialogue that involved contributions from many sides—science, anthropology and economics, along with philosophy, the involvements of the activist and the contemplation of the mystic, and the resources offered by the different theological and spiritual traditions. Likewise, the morality sustained by integral ecology does not look to the rigidly imposed ideology, but to the common good of all, life on earth as providence gives it for our joy, responsibility and care.

Into such a situation, the Father communicates the all-meaningful Word. The Word becomes flesh in the human conversation, to redeem it of bias and absurdity through the fullness of grace and

---

22. *STh* 1, 43, 4 ad 1.

truth (Jn 1:14). The Word incarnate in the life, death and resurrection of Christ, takes habitual worldviews by surprise and subverts the omnicompetent pretensions of human wisdom (Jn 3:1–10; 1 Cor 1:18–25). The non-violent presence of the truth not of this world is a judgment on the totalitarian violence of all human ideologies which, by denying God, end by mutilating humanity itself (Jn 18:36-38). The Word, as the self-expression of the love that God is (1 Jn 4), exists in the world as the 'light' in which all is judged. He comes into the world as 'the Word breathing love',[23] the universal love that has its origins in the heart of the Trinity.

With the Father as the horizon of the absolute future, and the Word incarnate as breathing forth love from the cross, the Spirit comes as God's original loving. God's indwelling loving inspires our hearing of the Word that has been uttered: 'No one can say, Jesus is Lord except by the Holy Spirit' (1 Cor 12:3). The Spirit inspires dreams in the old and visions in the young (Acts 2:17). The Paraclete, the Spirit of truth, glorifies Jesus and declares who he is and what he stands for to the disciples (Jn 16:12–15). By inspiring intimacy with God invoked as 'Abba' (Rom 8:15–16), the Spirit brings forth the fruits of self-transcendence in the believer (Gal 5:22) and in the Christian community (1 Cor 12:4–13). The love of God poured out by the Spirit gives assurance to the courageous practice of hope (Rom 5:5), within the groaning of all creation and the inward groanings of Christians. Indeed, the Spirit also 'groans', opening human consciousness to the mystery of love at work (Rom 8:19–28). Human values are renewed and informed by a Spirit-breathed love that 'bears all things, believes all things, hopes all things, endures all things' (1 Cor 13:7), in the love that never ends (v 8).

For those who would act in hope in the face of challenges inherent in becoming a global and planetary humanity, there is the ever-renewable resource of the gift of God: God is love—as the giver, the given and the giving. Though the mystery of the Trinity may not be explicitly named, it comes into the lives of many good people as an experience of a mysteriously radical and moving gift.

---

23. *STh* 1, 43, 5 ad 2.

In an appealing passage, Lonergan writes:

> There is in the world, as it were, a charged field of
> love and meaning; here and there it reaches a notable
> intensity; but it is every unobtrusive, hidden, inviting
> us to join. And join we must if we are to perceive it, for
> our perceiving is through our loving.[24]

In this sense, God, even as Trinity, is named from the experience of
a community of love embracing all in the name of God. In such a
perspective, the Church can be identified as that part of the world
that is expressly alive to the universal mystery of love at work.
Accordingly, it deals in words, signs, symbols and sacraments in
order to live and manifest the trinitarian mystery. In this respect,
the Church belongs within an 'ecology'[25]of divine presence and
communication, without limiting the total scope of God's grace at
work in all creation.

What are termed the divine invisible and visible missions to
the world arise from the trinitarian vitality of God. Today these
missions demand a re-expression from a dynamic and future-
directed perspective. In that regard, the 'invisible' missions are
invisible precisely because they energise the indefinable totality of the
universe. In that light, the emergent universe can be contemplated
in the light of one vast act of divine self-communication. In that
horizon, the self-giving God becomes the soul, the heart, the mind
of the world's emergence: 'There is . . . one God and Father of
all, who is above all and through all and in all' (Eph 4:6). On the
other hand, the *visibility* of the missions discloses the universe in
terms of divine incarnation. The divine mystery of Love incarnates
the Word in the body of creation as its form and goal. Love, too,
enters the world as the Spirit acts in all the self-giving activities that

---

24. Bernard Lonergan, *Method in Theology* (London: Darton, Longman and Todd, 1972),
    290.
25. Patristic and usual theological language speaks of the divine *economia*. I suggest that
    a better translation for this term in the present context is 'ecology'.

characterise our human and cosmic development. Further, as the Father is intimated as the source of both Word and Spirit, the world of time moves toward its absolute future in God.

We might say, therefore, that the trinitarian God is 'enworlded'. The divine communal life makes of the world a field of growing connections and relationships. The mind of the Word incarnate finds expression in the prayer of Jesus, 'As you, Father are in me, and I in you, may they also be in us . . . may they be one as we are one' (Jn 17:21–23). Then, there is the promise: 'When the Spirit of truth comes, he will guide you into all truth . . . and he will declare to you the things that are to come' (Jn 16:13).

Realism insistently demands recognition of the tragic world of conflicts and self-destruction in which we live. Whatever our ultimate hope, this is no one world of harmonious connections or gently conducted dialogue. We must realistically bear in mind that trinitarian grace in such a world must first of all be a force for healing and reconciling, before it is finally transforming. The energy of God's gifts—indeed of divine self-giving—is marked with the intensity of self-sacrifice. The missions of the Son and the Spirit are directed to human beings locked in an apparently insuperable problem of evil. The problem reaches a limit when the incarnation of the Word results in the crucifixion of the Father's beloved Son. The Father himself is revealed as having no self-disclosure in this world other than through the Crucified One. Similarly the Spirit of love and peace is sent into the self-enclosed world of violence. In that world of resistance, the Holy Spirit witnesses to no power and no truth other than that of the selfless love that is manifested in the Cross. In this way, through the incarnation and gift of the Spirit, God's presence in the world comes up against the power of evil. In that conflict, the self-giving love of God is exposed to the alienation, failure and fragmentation of our world; but so as to prove greater than the power of darkness: the crucified One is risen, and the Spirit has been poured out. The promise of transformation presumes that there is first of all a healing for the self-destructiveness manifest in human history.[26] God's communication is not reserved for pure spirits, but is concretely addressed to the vast drama of human history at the point where hope is failing.[27]

5. A Continuing Exploration

There is nothing new in exploring the transcendent reality of God by the way of analogy, that is, by appealing to what is more known in human experience in order to gain some knowledge of God. In Catholic tradition, Augustine's 'vestige' and 'image' doctrine[28] developed into the typically Franciscan cosmic sense of all reality sacramentally manifesting God. For example, over seven hundred years ago, Robert Grosseteste, the first Chancellor of the University of Oxford, contemplating a speck of dust, finds, in its existence, form and goodness, a manifestation of the three divine persons.[29] Now, a speck of dust caught in the light beaming in through a medieval scholar's window is rather different from other specks we know today. For example, the earth is a mere speck in a universe of some hundred billion galaxies. Indeed, the Big Bang suggests the unfolding of the cosmos through 14.7 billion years from the infinitesimal super-compressed 'speck' of its beginnings. In a trinitarian perspective, and in continuity with the past, Christian faith can contemplate the originality, the dynamic form, the wonder and beauty of life on earth and its cosmic connections. Likewise, St Bonaventure, in his ladder of contemplation, could consider creation as implying a trinitarian presence on three ascending rungs of intensity. First, there are 'footprints' (*vestigia*) of the Creator found in the pre-personal. Second, there is the divine 'image' in the spiritual creature with its powers of intelligence and love. Third, there is the divine similitude or 'likeness' brought about as the created spirit is transformed through grace:

---

26. See Kelly, *Trinity of Love*, 168f; 195–202.
27. *STh* I, q. 43, a. 7; q. 88, a. 3.
28. *De Trinitate* VI; VIII-XV.
29. Servus Gieben, 'Traces of God in Nature according to Robert Grosseteste', in *Franciscan Studies* XXIV (1964): 154–6.

The creation of the world as a book in which the creative Trinity shines forth. It is read according to the three levels of expression, the ways of vestige, image and likeness. By these, as up a ladder's steps, the human intellect has the power to climb by stages to the supreme principle which is God.[30]

Laudato Si' invokes this long theological tradition:

For Christians, the Trinity has left its mark on all creation. Bonaventure teaches us that *each creature bears in itself a specifically Trinitarian structure*, so real that it could be readily contemplated if only the human gaze were not so partial, dark and fragile. In this way, he points out to us the challenge of trying to read reality in a Trinitarian key [239].

There are two points to be made:

1. Christian contemplation envisages not only the Word made flesh in the Incarnation, thus claiming the world as his own, but also the world 'trinified' and possessed by each of the divine persons. The Trinity is present in the world, and is held in its being in the mind and heart of the Trinity. It is thus caught up and carried forward in the Trinitarian life, and finds its final transformation in the Trinitarian God

2. 'To read reality in a trinitarian key' is to interpret the world and the signs of the times against a trinitarian horizon. God is communicating the divine self to the world in the unifying love of the Spirit, in the ever deeper understanding that indicates the presence of the Word, with a sense of all embracing and abiding mystery arising out of the wonder of life.

---

30. Bonaventure, *Intinerarium Mentis in Deum* c. 3, n. 5.

For most of Christian reflection on the Trinity in relation to the world, the implied metaphor was a stable ladder of being, with God at the top and material realities on the lowest rung—with human beings somewhere around the middle. This metaphor of ascending rungs tends now to be replaced by the arrow of time moving forward in an evolutionary direction. The 'footprints' or traces of God now have to be tracked in the history of the billions of years of the world's emergence. Then, the divine image is disclosed in terms of human consciousness emerging in such an evolutionary world so that world becomes known and appreciated in the human mind and heart as the gift of the Creator. The higher 'likeness' of God, in its turn, is revealed in the transformation of consciousness as it inhabited by the primordial mystery of creative Love.

Aquinas sums up the themes of the great Greek theologians, especially Athanasius and Gregory of Nyssa, when he treats of the presence of the Trinity in the act of creation:

> [T]he divine persons are causes of the creation of things in the order of their procession, since God acts from his knowledge and will as a craftsman acts in regard to what he produces. The craftsman acts through a word conceived in his mind and through love in his will in reference to what is to be made. Hence the Father creates through his Word which is the Son, and through his Love which is the Spirit.[31]

In such a vision, the trinitarian mystery is implicit in what it means to be a creature. Moreover, the trinitarian processions of Word and Spirit are at the foundations of the cosmic process. Indeed, Aquinas goes on to say that

> The knowledge of the divine persons is necessary for us for two reasons: in the first place, to have a right sense of the creation of things. Because we say that God

---

31. *STh* I, q. 45, a. 6, ad 2.

created all things by his Word, the error is excluded of holding that God produced things out of the necessity of his nature. Because we hold that there is a procession of love within him, it is clear that God did not produce creatures out of some extrinsic need, but on account of love for his goodness... In the second place, and this is more important, [the Trinity is disclosed] that we might have a proper sense of the salvation of the human race, which is brought about by the incarnation of the Son and through the gift of the Holy Spirit.[32]

That 'right sense of creation' implies that creation is not a divine necessity. It is an act of love, a communication from the heart of God. Secondly, the 'salvation of the human race' results from God's self-giving to human beings within the historical and evolutionary dynamics of their world. In continuity with its traditional methods, trinitarian theology remains free to exploit new resources of language and experience to explicate the trinitarian form of creation. It must explore the variety of ways in which the presence of the trinitarian God can be discerned within a relational and evolutionary perspective. In so doing, a reflective faith is coming to a fuller insight into the deeper implications of its central mystery. For instance, Beatrice Bruteau remarked:

The cosmos has all the marks of the Trinity: it is a unity; it is internally differentiated but interpenetrating; and it is dynamic, giving, expansive, radiant. And, as a work of art, the cosmos has another important character: it does not exist for the sake of something else, something beyond itself; it is not useful, it is not instrumental; it is an end in itself, self-justifying, valuable in its own right and in its very process. This, I think, is foundational for . . . ecological virtue . . .[33]

---

32. *STh* I, q. 32, a. 1, ad 3.
33. Beatrice Bruteau, 'Eucharistic Ecology and Ecological Spirituality', in *Cross Currents*

Ecological virtue is sustained by trinitarian contemplation of creation. To experience God in such a way is to find oneself as a 'connected self', a self-to-be-realised in relationship to the other. This 'other' today admits of a global, ecological, and cosmic extension. Trinitarian faith orientates the believer into a world of relationship and communion. It implies an agenda for the transformation of ourselves, our communities, our global co-existence:[34] There can be found here the basic ecumenism of a faith grounded in the mystery of the Trinity and earthed in ecological awareness.[35] As Beatrice Bruteau remarked, 'the cosmos has all the marks of the Trinity' in its unity, internal differentiation and in the dynamics of its expansion and interrelatedness.[36]

A vivid sense of the trinitarian dimension of human existence profoundly affects the lived sense of human selfhood. Christian theology speaks of the divine indwelling. It is at once God dwelling in us, and ourselves dwelling in God. To search into who we are is to find ourselves in the presence of God, the Self in all our selves, and the life in all our lives. Life is healed and expanded in the trinitarian communion of truth and love, while the mystery of the Trinity overflows into the wonder of creation. In this trinitarian perspective, creation arises from the original giving of the Father, shows forth the expressiveness of the Word, and lives and moves to fulfillment through the Spirit.

As Pope Francis remarks,

> This leads us not only to marvel at the manifold connections but also to discover a key to our own fulfilment. The human person grows more, matures more and is sanctified more to the extent that he or she enters into relationships, going out from themselves to live in communion with God, with others and with

---

(Winter 1990): 504.

34. Anne Hunt, *Trinity: Nexus of the Mysteries of Trinitarian Faith* (Maryknoll, NY: Orbis, 2005), 104–114.

35. Denis Edwards, *Ecology at the Heart of Faith*, 65–80.

36. Bruteau, 'Eucharistic Ecology and Ecological Spirituality', 504.

all creatures—that trinitarian dynamism which God imprinted in them when they were created. Everything is interconnected, and this invites us to develop a spirituality of that global solidarity which flows from the mystery of the Trinity [240].

In such a spirituality, it is presumed that,

1. Fulfilment occurs through relationship to the other, i.e., to God, our neighbor and the neighbourhood of our common home;
2. A global solidarity flows from, participates in, and finds its ultimate fulfilment in the mystery of the Trinity
3. Spirituality is the habitual disposition of finite human consciousness to live in the presence of God, so to find all things in God, the whole of creation as a gift.

Conclusion

Christian language refers to the divine indwelling, with the implications that God dwells in us, and we dwell in God. The three classic biblical expressions of such intimacy with the divine mystery are familiar. We are *temples* of the Holy Spirit, *members* of the Body of Christ, and *children* of the Father. Through this indwelling and union with the divine persons, faith possesses an inside knowledge of the mystery of the Trinity by participating in the innermost life of God. It shares in the Love-Life that God is:

Beloved, let us love one another, because love is from God; everyone who loves is born of God and knows God . . . For God is love . . . No one has ever seen God; if we love one another, God lives in us and his love is perfected in us (1 Jn 4:7–12).

In conclusion, the words of a great mystic which sum up the points we have laboured to make, namely that truly integral ecology is deeply trinitarian:

> O eternal Trinity, fire and abyss of charity . . . by the light of understanding within your light I have tasted and seen your depth . . . and the beauty of your creation. Then, when I considered myself in you, I saw that I am your image. You have gifted me with power from yourself, and my understanding with your wisdom— such wisdom as is proper to your only-begotten Son; and the Holy Spirit who proceeds from you and your Son, has given me a will, and so I am able to love.[37]

To experience God in such a way is to find oneself as a relational identity; we are each a self-to-be-realised in relationship to the other: 'It has not yet appeared who we shall be' (1 Jn 3:2). Adoration of God and union with the divine persons orient the believer into a world of relationships and communion—of global, ecological, and cosmic dimensions. In that sense, the Trinity implies an agenda for conversion and transformation, for ourselves, our communities, and our global co-existence. In a world both of complex differentiation and growing interconnectedness, Christian faith can find a new health and a new wholeness in contemplating the universe in the light of its fundamental mystery—the Trinity gathering creation to itself. In the Trinity, the universe comes home; and all the struggling emergence of time finds its absolute future. Through such trinitarian reflections our exploration into God comes to rely on God's own 'inside knowledge' as it is revealed to faith.

---

37. St Catherine of Siena, *The Dialogues*, translated by Suzanne Loffke, OP, *The Classics of Western Spirituality* (New York: Paulist Press, 1980), 365.

Chapter Five:
A Eucharistic Ecology

How might the Eucharist shape an ecological vision? Nagging ecological questions need answers: Can respect for nature find its proper place in a technologically driven and consumer-oriented culture? Must human culture always be at the expense of natural world? Is that natural world preserved only by banishing the human presence as destructive and parasitical?

1. Cultural Dislocation

Answers are not easy to find when, clearly, the great emancipations of the modern age have had to pay a particularly heavy price. In the struggle against what was perceived to be oppressive tradition or archaic order or biological limitations, forms of liberation have meant leaving much behind. The modern emancipated individual is uprooted from a sense of nature that meant only limitation and even threat. To that degree, individual freedom became detached from a sense of a sacred nurturing universe. Since that larger, englobing mystery of things was perceived to be outside the range of human control, freedom was not a matter of surrendering to that greater mysterious whole, but of defining oneself against it, and as apart from it. Mircea Eliade remarks,

> As for the Christianity of the industrial societies and especially the Christianity of intellectuals, it has long since lost the cosmic values it still possessed in the Middle Ages. The cosmic liturgy, the mystery of nature's participation in the christological drama, have become

111

> inaccessible to Christians living in a modern city . . . at
> most we recognise that we are responsible to God and
> also to history—but the world is no longer felt as the
> work of God.[1]

When we no longer feel that the world is the work of God, an
extreme alienation is possible. Nonetheless—and this is what Eliade
does not grant—there remain ever-renewable resources of Christian
vision and sensibility typically available in the Eucharist. In a more
'enlightened' Enlightenment, such resources can be retrieved, but,
this time, in a way that will be less rationalistic, less anthropocentric
and individual, and more attuned to a participation in nature and
its cosmic dimensions. Indeed, a cosmic connection was part of
the deep sensibility of Christian tradition—as any familiarity with
the Eastern Fathers, and the great medieval doctors, St Thomas
Aquinas and St Bonaventure, clearly shows. But with the loss of that
sense of connection, the world appeared as a limitless resource to be
explored, harnessed, exploited, and consumed for all the varieties of
human purpose.

The modern mind, even that of Christian believers, needs
therefore to recover a sense both of planetary environment and the
cosmic whole. Neither a return to ancient science nor a rejection
of modern achievements are acceptable alternatives. But what
is required is a larger and more humble reinterpretation of the
traditional declaration of Ash Wednesday, 'Remember that you are
but dust and unto dust you shall return' (Gen 3:19). Now, however,
that 'dust' can be understood as a cosmic reality since we are 'made
of stardust'. Our bodies are distillations of the cosmic matter and
energies that make up the physical universe over the billions of years
of its emergence. We humans are embodied in a cosmic totality.
What then is the Eucharistic connection?

---

1. Mircea Eliade, *The Sacred and the Profane. The Nature of Religion*, translated by
   Willard R Trask (New York: Harcourt, Brace and World,1959), 179.

2. Eucharistic Ecology

The Eucharist, however, inspires a genuinely integral ecology. It brings nature and culture together precisely by relating them to the Body of Christ. The 'real presence' of the whole Christ is communicated to the community through the transformation of the shared 'fruit of the earth and the work of human hands'. Through the power of the Spirit, the bread becomes our 'bread of life', just as the wine that is offered becomes 'our spiritual drink'. Thus, the earthy elements that sustain human life and communication have an essential place in the 'ecology' of God's self-giving in Christ. A precious point emerges: unless creation is radically from God, it could not figure so intrinsically in God's self-giving relationship to the world.

In this respect, the Eucharist brings together many gifts and many forms of giving. It offers to all who would receive it a holy communion within a universe of grace and giving. From nature's giving we have the grain and the grapes. From the giving expressed in human work and skill, we have the gifts of bread and wine. From the generous giving of family and friends flow the gifts of good meals and festive celebrations. From Jesus' self-giving at the Last Supper, the disciples were given his 'body and blood', the food and drink to nourish life in him. He will breathe into his disciples the gift of the Spirit. And working in and through all these gifts and modes of giving is the gift of the Father who so loved the world. When the Church celebrates the Eucharist, all these gifts come together to nourish our lives in this world with the gift of communion with God.[2]

This is not without significance for Christians responding to the present ecological challenges. Problems are compounded by the artificiality of modern technological culture, as already noted. The human has been effectively uprooted humanity from nature. For its part, the Eucharist inspires a more humble and far reaching

---

2. John D Zizioulas, *The Eucharistic Communion and the World*, edited by Luke Ben Tallon (London: T&T Clark, 2011), 128–131; 135–140; 151–154.

wisdom. The richness of sacramentality stimulates an expansively catholic imagination, as an 'openness to the whole' (*kat'holou*) in a full communal and inclusive sense. As a result, a God-centred totality comes to expression in which each part lives in the whole, and the whole is present in each part. To celebrate this sacrament in the time and space of human existence is to confess that 'God was in Christ reconciling the world to himself' (2 Cor 5:19).

3. Body and Spirit, Nature and Grace

In a telling paragraph, Pope Francis writes:

> The Sacraments are a privileged way in which nature is taken up by God to become a means of mediating supernatural life. Through our worship of God, we are invited to embrace the world on a different plane. Water, oil, fire and colours are taken up in all their symbolic power and incorporated in our act of praise. This is especially clear in the spirituality of the Christian East. For Christians, all the creatures of the material universe find their true meaning in the incarnate Word, for the Son of God has incorporated in his person part of the material world, planting in it a seed of definitive transformation. 'Christianity does not reject matter. Rather, bodiliness is considered in all its value in the liturgical act, whereby the human body is disclosed in its inner nature as a temple of the Holy Spirit and is united with the Lord Jesus, who himself took a body for the world's salvation'[3] [235].

We can single out four points in the above paragraph especially relevant to a Christian integral ecology:

---

3. Here Pope Francis is quoting John Paul II, Apostolic Letter *Orientale Lumen* (May 2, 1995),11, in *AAS* 87 (1995), 757.

1. A condensed theology of the sacraments is background for the treatment of the Eucharist: The Sacraments are a privileged way in which nature is taken up by God to become a means of mediating supernatural life. Nature supplies not only 'the matter of the sacraments', but also, from a larger perspective, suggests what might be termed 'the sacramentality of matter'.

2. Through our Christian worship of God, faith embraces the world on a different plane. Water, oil, fire, bread and wine, colours, scents and human gestures are taken up in all their symbolic power and incorporated in the act of praise and thanksgiving.

3. All creatures of the material universe find their true meaning in the incarnate Word, for the Son of God has embodied the material world in his person, planting in it a seed of definitive transformation.

4. Christianity does not reject matter in the name of some higher spirituality. Rather, faith and worship are expressed in and through our bodies. In the liturgy itself, the human body is disclosed in its true nature as a temple of the Holy Spirit and is united with the Lord Jesus who, as the Word incarnate on this earth, embodies the world to come.

The Eucharist, then, provides a generous framework in which to sustain ecological thinking and action. It leads to thanksgiving, *eucharistia*, for the gifts of God given in and to this present world of time and space. It does not defer to a future indifferent to what we now are. Our earth, our flesh and blood—all this matters to God's creative purpose. Our future in God is not designed to empty us of what we already are. In the Christian perspective, we flesh and blood human beings are, indeed, fed with the Bread of Heaven and filled with the energies of the Spirit. This nourishment occurs through the consecration of the bread and wine made from the wheat and the grapes that this terrestrial ecology has produced.

The fruitfulness of the earth unfolds in history. As the Christmas antiphon sings, 'Let the earth be open to bud forth the saviour!' The Holy Spirit working through Mary, this woman of both Israel and the earth, brings forth Jesus Christ, the Son of God, to be the son of Mary, to breathe the air of planet Earth. Jesus, in his love unto the end, in his death and resurrection, draws creation into the trinitarian life, as he prays to the Father, 'May they be one, as we are one' (Jn 17:22). The longing of the human spirit unfolds in an horizon already filled with the creative, self-giving love of God. The divine Spirit works to form all humanity and our world into the Body of Christ.

Moved by the Spirit, Christian faith blossoms into its sacramental imagination: symbols, gestures, words, relationships and biological processes of our world come to be appreciated, in their respective ritual forms, as 'visible signs of invisible grace' (Augustine). Such sacramental actions culminate in the Eucharist as the risen Lord, Christ takes fragments of creation, elements of our earthly reality which nature and history have combined to produce, in order to transform them into something more, in anticipation of a new totality: 'This is my body; this is my blood. . . .' Jesus' transforming identification with the matter of our world is continued through history in each Eucharistic gathering: 'Do this in memory of me'. For Christians to receive the Eucharistic gift of the body and blood of Jesus is to claim this world as their own in the way that Christ already possesses it. In so doing, we become immeasurably larger selves in a world in which the Word made flesh dwells amongst us. The result is not some vague form of pantheism, but the cosmic dimensions of the Incarnation itself. By assuming our humanity, the divine Word necessarily possesses the world and universe in which humanity exists. Celebrated within a process of cosmic transformation,[4] the Eucharist offers a humble and far reaching

---

4.   Peter C Phan, 'Eschatology and Ecology: The Environment in the End-Time', in *Irish Theological Quarterly*, 62 (1996): 3–16.

wisdom, bringing together what is too often kept apart: nature and culture, the individual and the community, creation and God. [5]

4. From the Imagination of Jesus

The Eucharist arises from the imagination of Jesus himself, intent on communicating true life to the world (Jn 10:10). With the arrival of the hour in which God's universal love will be revealed, the meaning of the Eucharist comes into focus (Jn 13:1–17). In this respect, John 6, referring to Jesus as the bread of life, must be read in conjunction with John 13, and the example and commandment that he gives.[6] In this respect, God is not an object to be possessed by connoisseurs of religious experience, but the mystery of self-giving love expressed in Jesus washing the disciples' feet. What most characterises the divine life is love for the other. For Jesus, the Father himself is the Other to whom he is turned. But in turning to the Father, the Son is impelled to give himself for all whom God loves, the many others, the disciples and those who will believe through their witness. The way of Jesus, in ascending upward to the Father, is necessarily outward to the world. He washes the disciples' feet. The supreme moment of love is not an escape from the world but a deeper involvement with it. This remains an always disconcerting dimension in Christian life. The Eucharist, even as it praises and glorifies God, demands mutual love and service amongst those who celebrate it. As they turn with the Son to face the Father they are inescapably faced with the all-too-familiar other, as the neighbour appears in a taken-for-granted environment. But this other is to be loved and served in accord with Jesus' example and his new commandment. To love God means loving others; worshipping the Father entails dedication to all God's children, our brothers and sisters, and to the earthly home we have in common. The Father's house (Jn 14:2) into which Jesus

---

5. For a sophisticated discussion of the modern situation and the value of the Eucharist, see Simon Oliver, 'The Eucharist Before Nature and Culture', in *Modern Theology* 15/3 (July 1999): 331–353.
6. See Francis J Moloney, SDB, *The Gospel of John, Sacra Pagina,* vol 4, Daniel Harrington, SJ, Editor (Collegeville, MN: The Liturgical Press, 1998), especially 372–378.

goes to prepare a place for his followers, breathes an overwhelming hospitality. He lays down the rules of God's household by washing his disciples' feet, and exhorting them to do likewise. In the realm of the Father, love rules.

In a vision formed by the Eucharist, everything is changed. God can no longer be kept in place, confined to heaven, for the Father has sent his Son into the world. With the coming of Jesus, the world itself loses its self-made boundaries. Heaven is opened (Jn 1:51). Nor can Jesus be kept in his place, for he is leaving this world for the Father. Even death ceases to be an opaque impenetrable limit. Jesus' death will be a 'lifting up', the event in which the love of God will be revealed. In the glory of this love, the disciples too must move beyond the limits that selfishness, fear or grief might impose. Jesus's going to the Father draws his disciples with him into a universe of love. No believer can ever live again in self-contained isolation: 'Just as I have loved you, you also should love one another' (Jn 13:34). His real presence in the food and drink of the Eucharist demands that it be also a true presence in the hearts and conduct of his followers in the world whose air they breathe, and whose soil has produced the wheat and grapes that the Eucharist will consecrate.

An ecological and Eucharistic imagination arises with the conviction that human beings are creatures of this earth and stewards of God's good creation. Indeed, the most intense moment of the Church's communion with God is at the same time an intense moment of our communion with the earth. Thus, the sacramental elements anticipate the cosmic transformation that is afoot, not as leaving the created cosmos behind, but as anticipating its healing and transformation. [7]

This Eucharistic vision is an important Christian inspiration to ecological virtue. Respect for the diversity of life and the wonder of this unique biosphere needs more than purely a scientific analysis. The ever-renewable resources of faith, hope and love have a part to play in the appreciation of life and in the conservation of the planet's

---

7. On this cosmic transformation in Christ, see Denis Edwards, *Ecology at the Heart of Faith*, 82–98; 122.

non-renewal resources. Furthermore, the Eucharistic envisions a cosmic transformation of all things in Christ. It thus counters a naive ecological ideology which imagines nature in the past as an unspoilt and innocent state. On the other hand, a doctrinaire evolutionary ideology can empty the significance of the present into an impersonal and incalculable future. The most intense moment of communion with God is at the same time an intense moment of our communion with the earth as 'the fruit of the earth and the works of human hands' arso given as to become 'true food and true drink' (Jn 6:55).

'Transubstantiated' in this way, the sacramental elements anticipate the cosmic transformation that is afoot, not as something that leaves the created cosmos behind, but as promising its healing and transformation.

5. An Ever-Renewable Resource

A positive vision is one of the important ingredients that Christian faith can offer to ecological awareness. Our day is marked with an increasing appreciation of the diversity of life and with a concern to protect the unique wonder of our biosphere. But something more than a purely scientific calculation is needed. A more integrated sense of the whole is needed. The cosmic scale of the Eucharist is powerfully evoked in the following paragraph for *Laudato Si'*:

> It is in the Eucharist that all that has been created finds its greatest exaltation. Grace, which tends to manifest itself tangibly, found unsurpassable expression when God himself became man and gave himself as food for his creatures. The Lord, in the culmination of the mystery of the Incarnation, chose to reach our intimate depths through a fragment of matter. He comes not from above, but from within, he comes that we might find him in this world of ours. In the Eucharist, fullness is already achieved; it is the living centre of the universe, the overflowing core of love and of inexhaustible life.

Joined to the incarnate Son, present in the Eucharist, the whole cosmos gives thanks to God. Indeed the Eucharist is itself an act of cosmic love: 'Yes, cosmic! Because even when it is celebrated on the humble altar of a country church, the Eucharist is always in some way celebrated on the altar of the world'. [8]The Eucharist joins heaven and earth; it embraces and penetrates all creation. The world which came forth from God's hands returns to him in blessed and undivided adoration: in the bread of the Eucharist, 'creation is projected towards divinization, towards the holy wedding feast, towards Union with the Creator himself' [236].

We emphasise six points in this paragraph:

1. 'It is in the Eucharist that all that has been created finds its greatest exaltation'.
2. 'Grace, which tends to manifest itself tangibly, found unsurpassable expression when God himself became man and gave himself as food for his creatures'.
3. 'The Lord, in the culmination of the mystery of the Incarnation, chose to reach our intimate depths through a fragment of matter. He comes not from above, but from within, he comes that we might find him in this world of ours'.
4. 'In the Eucharist, fullness is already achieved; it is the living centre of the universe, the overflowing core of love and of inexhaustible life'.
5. 'Joined to the incarnate Son, present in the Eucharist, the whole cosmos gives thanks to God. Indeed, the Eucharist is itself an act of cosmic love celebrated on the altar of the world'.

---

8. Citing John Paul II, Encyclical Letter *Ecclesia de Eucharistia* (17 April, 2003), 8: *AAS* 95 (2003), 438.

6. 'The Eucharist joins heaven and earth; it embraces and penetrates all creation. The world which came forth from God's hands returns to him in blessed and undivided adoration: in the bread of the Eucharist, 'creation is projected towards divinization, towards the holy wedding feast, towards union with the Creator himself' (John Paul II).

With these points in mind, we can take a further step. Catholic tradition employs the hallowed term, transubstantiation, to indicate the manner in which the bread and wine are changed into the Lord's body and blood. This doctrinal element of the sacramental tradition is, however, in need of a larger cosmic perspective, as when it is realised that the Eucharist is being celebrated within a cosmic process of transformation.[9] The physical, the chemical, the biological structures of our universe have culminated, through a succession of transformations, in human consciousness. In our minds and hearts, the universe has become aware of itself as vast wonderful mystery. Within it, we live and breathe, humbly aware that we are not the centre or origin of all this great cosmic event, but thankful for the sheer gift of existence, patient and hopeful as it catches us up and carries us forward.

The great world of nature has brought us forth to exist now as spiritual beings. We are able to think and act, to love and hope and pray. We arise out of nature, but are not contained by it. For now there is an even larger span, the openness, the creativity and the freedom of spirit and soul. We possess the freedom to live in a spiritual horizon and so to freely determine the direction of our lives and to shape the environment in which we live. At the very least, this is to experience this marvellous, unfinished and restless humanity as a question: Are we to live on the earth, enjoying what it offers and suffering through what it imposes, finally to die, yet to remain through it all, spiritually unconscious? Is the question

---

9. For a seminal work, see Gustave Martelet, *The Risen Christ and the Eucharist World*, translated by René Hague (New York: Crossroad, 1976).

of the origin and goal of all this gift too big or too threatening to pose? Who, what, is the giver of all these gifts? Are we to take our existence for granted, so to understand ourselves in the end, to be merely as consumers, even on a cosmic scale?

On the other hand, we owe our existence to the Other, the great creative mystery that has brought us into being. Are we to live on this earth through which we have received much, but as having no part of the giving, as life-givers, love-givers, care-givers for the generations to come?

To be in any way touched by such questions is to live in an expanding horizon of wonder and gratitude. In this created universe, what does its creator intend for us? What are we to do with ourselves as the stream of life lifts us up, carries us on, and confronts us with the fact that we were not here until very recently, and will not be here, forever? The span of human history (two hundred thousand years?) and the eight decades or so of any given life, are only the merest instant in the fifteen thousand million years that have gone into the making of our world. And yet, as has been so well said, 'We are nature's big chance to become spirited'.[10]

Eucharistic faith brings to expression the scope and shape of our humanity. It presupposes all the material and biological transformations that peak in the emergence of human consciousness. It carries forward to the momentous leap in human history that occurred in Israel's special covenant with the One God. Then, Mary's Spirit-inspired 'Let it be with me according to your word' (Lk 1:38) embodies the genetic potential of creation. She gives her consent to become pregnant with the Christ, the final 'life-form' of creation, yet sharing in the life of this planet.

As the Spirit of Christ animates our humanity, faith blossoms into its sacramental imagination: symbols, gestures, words, relationships and biological processes of our world come to be appreciated in different sacramental contexts as 'visible signs of invisible grace'.

---

10. A happy phrase borrowed from David S Toolan's own splendidly 'spirited reflection', 'Nature is an Heraclitean Fire. Reflections on Cosmology in and Ecological Age', in *Studies in the Spirituality of the Jesuits* 23/5 (November 1991): 36.

These reach their most intense and comprehensive form in the Eucharist. The risen Lord takes to himself elements of our earthly reality which nature and history have combined to produce, in order to transform them into something more, in anticipation of a new totality: 'This is my body; this is my blood . . . '. Jesus' transforming identification with the matter of our world continues through history as the Eucharist is celebrated: 'Do this in memory of me'. The Lord invites us to connect with the cosmos as he has done. By receiving the Eucharistic gift of his body and blood, we are in fact claiming this world as our own in the way that Christ already possesses it. We thus become immeasurably larger selves in a world of divine incarnation. We are not here commending some vague form of pantheism, but recognising the effect of the Incarnation itself as it makes us see the world as the 'body' of God.[11] By assuming our humanity, the divine Word necessarily makes his own the world and universe to which that humanity is essentially related.

6. Eucharistic Contemplation

Both Greek philosophy and Hebrew faith strongly distinguished between God and the world, between the Creator and creation. The distinctively Christian faith in the incarnation of the Word brings together what even the deepest philosophy and the greatest faith had hitherto kept apart. The sacrament of the Eucharist implies that God is so much God, so limitless and creative in goodness, that the divine Spirit can so reach into the innermost depths of matter as to give the physical world a part in communicating the most divine of gifts. From another point of view, the material world is so much deeply and fully created by God, so possessed and held in being by the Creator, that it is the medium through which God contacts us. Thus, the Word became flesh and dwelt amongst us. The sacramental imagination of the Church affirms in fact that not only bread and wine, water and oil and human gestures figure in the sacraments, but also human sexuality—as in the sacrament of marriage. When

---

11. Hans Urs von Balthasar, *The Glory of the Lord*, 679.

the Eucharist along with other sacraments, celebrate the intimacy of God present and working in creation, this is far from being a regression to mythological thinking but it is recognising the singular reality of the incarnation. The universe comes into being through the Word, and finds its coherence and full reality in him: 'He was in the beginning with God. All things came into being through him, and without him not one thing came into being. What has come into being in him was life, and the life was the light of all people' (Jn 1:2–4).

The range of Christian faith is always expanding. The great mystics witness to the indwelling intimacy and extent of God's presence in the universe.[12] In their sense of the utter otherness of God, contemplatives first undergo a purifying withdrawal from the created world. But their detachment is preliminary to openness and surrender. An example of this 'way of negation' is John of the Cross' repeated *nada*, 'nothing, nothing, nothing . . . and even on the mountain nothing'.[13] It leads to emptiness and silence. Beyond all human conceptions, images and projections, faith experiences a kind of spiritual nakedness before the all-surpassing mystery of God alone. To pray is to enter into this 'cloud of unknowing'; to attend to 'a sound of sheer silence; (1 Kgs 19:12). The believer must be 'nakedly intent' on the divine will, and surrendered to it, lost in it alone, beyond the clamour of needs and desires.

But then the illumination! In going up the mountain of ascent, we meet the Other coming down into the plains of creation. God is ever creating the world, and ourselves within it, to make us hear his Word more fully and to receive his Spirit more deeply. To Philip's request, 'Lord, show us the Father and we will be satisfied', Jesus asks in his turn, 'Have I been with you all this time, Philip, and you still do not know me? Whoever has seen me, has seen the Father'

---

12. See Beatrice Bruteau, 'Eucharistic Ecology and Ecological Spirituality', in *Cross Currents* (Winter 1990): 499–514, for a profound meditation on the relevance of classic Christian doctrines to ecological awareness.
13. See *Vida y Obras de San Juan de la Cruz*, edited by Crisogono de Jesus (Madrid: Biblioteca de Autores Cristianos, 1955), 492.

(Jn 14:8f). But even this 'seeing' discloses perspectives beyond the scope of human vision and control. There is a play of darkness and light: '. . . if I do not go away, the Advocate will not come to you; but if I go, I will send him to you' (Jn 16:8). In this play of absence (the earthly departure of Jesus) and presence (his return through his gift of the Spirit), faith must maintain its buoyancy. Christ is present in the concrete earthly reality of the world into which the Word has come in the flesh, and to which the Spirit is sent. Jesus promises, 'I will do whatever you ask in my name, so that the Father will be glorified in the Son. If in my name you ask anything, I will do it' (Jn 14:13–14). In Christian prayer, creation awakens to its original mystery.

The Father's house is a home of 'many dwelling places' (Jn 14:2). Even as we live and breathe in this world, we can still follow Jesus into our particular 'dwelling place', as we pray and open our hearts to God's goodness revealed in all things. In the depth and breadth of prayer, the universe is revealed, not as an anonymous milieu, indifferent to life or death, but the homeland and heartland of God. Admittedly, this world can appear to be anonymous and indifferent as scientists tell of its enormous space and the billions of years that have gone into its making. The disciplined objectivity of science, intent on delineating the structure of the physical universe, speaks in an idiom that can easily make human beings feel that their presence here is purely the result of blind impersonal chance. But the scientific productions of the human mind achieve a strange outcome when they leave no room for the human heart. Science would hardly be a success story if it prevented us from appreciating the wonder of the cosmos as the homeland both of God, and also of humanity itself. It would be a distortion of science if it ignored the most obvious and astonishing phenomenon, human consciousness itself. If science gives in to a purely materialistic bias in the name of dispassionate objectivity, it leaves the world without fundamental meaning and value. In that case, the scientific mind might somehow haunt the immense complex universe, but would hardly inhabit it.

In contrast, the Eucharistic imagination adds a deeper sense of mystery to the so-called impersonal objectivity of science. In a Eucharistic context, the scientifically imagined universe comes to recognise another dimension, that of being the outcome of divine creation and incarnation. It is a space of communication with the God who has called the world into being. The Father has sent his Son to dwell amongst us. The Holy Spirit makes us aware of the great mystery at work. The Word incarnate owns our sufferings through the cross, and his resurrection from the dead inspires in us even now the hope of a final, universal transformation.

By nourishing minds and hearts with such mysteries, the Eucharist celebrates the universe as a great spiritual breathing space. In that God-filled space, everything and everyone is related. The Eucharistic universe does not suffocate the life of the world, but is immeasurably hospitable to all that it is. In this regard, the Eucharist educates the imagination, mind and heart to apprehend the universe as one of communion and connectedness in Christ. That totality is materialised in the earthly, physical elements of the shared bread and wine of the sacrament, in the community of believers receiving it, and in Christ giving himself to them as their food and drink. In that holy communion, the universe comes home to us as a new creation.

Through the Eucharist, the totality of creation is reclaimed as belonging to Christ, and to all who are 'in Christ'. Contemplative faith brings together the superficial, fragmented, and alienating elements, and lifts our experience into another vision. The universe is 'otherwise'; it is christened, and seeded with the Spirit-energies of faith, hope and love. It is being transformed 'transubstantiated'— into the Body of the Risen One. To this hopeful vision, the Body of Christ becomes the milieu of our existence, in which nothing is left out and nothing left behind. Eucharistic faith lives in the world of shared mystery, charged with communication, a field of relationships to everything and everyone. Though we human beings have been busy through our short history in sundering relationships to one another, to creation itself and to the Creator, the Divine Word has been writing our collective name in the dust of the earth we share as our common home. For 'in Christ'—according to the Pauline vision—all things hold together (Col 1:17), and are gathered up in him (Eph 1:10). Though he is the 'image of the invisible God', he is also 'the firstborn of all creation' (Col 1: 15). All things are made 'in him', and are destined to be 'for him' (v 16). The mystery of Christ is for the universe the all-unifying attractor, the direction inscribed into its origin, the goal drawing it onward, and the force holding it together. All reality—the physical world, all forms of life, human consciousness, its cultural creations, and its transformation in the Spirit—all are embodied in the plenitude of the Risen One. As the heart and centre of a transformed creation, he is the life and the light of the world (Jn 1:3–4).

Through the Eucharistic imagination, a distinctive ecological vision and commitment take shape. If the literal meaning of *eucharistia* is 'thanksgiving', the comprehensive meaning of such thanksgiving is found in gratitude for all the kinds of givings and gifts that nourish our existence. The self-giving love of the Father is the origin: 'In this is love, not that we loved God, but that he loved us and sent his Son to be the atoning sacrifice for our sins' (1 Jn 4:10). Paul begins his letter to the Ephesians with a great 'Eucharistic' outpouring:

> Blessed be the God and Father of our Lord Jesus Christ, who has blessed us in Christ with every spiritual blessing in the heavenly places, just as he chose us in Christ before the foundation of the world to be holy and blameless before him in love . . With all wisdom and insight he has made known to us the mystery of his will... as a plan for the fullness of time to gather up all things in him, things in heaven and things on earth (Eph 1:3–10).

The Father's primordial love is displayed in an all-comprehending providence. The 'one God and Father of all, who is above all and through all and in all' (Eph 4:6) is ever at work for our sake, gathering up all things in Christ, the 'things of heaven and things of earth'.

Whether our gaze is upward to God, or outward and downward to the earth, we are confronted with so many dimensions of God's giving. We are indeed 'up to our necks in debt'.[14] Divine providence has guided the great cosmic processes over billions of years to create the conditions in which planet earth could be a biosphere, a place of life. The same providence has worked through the evolutionary dynamics that have made us what we are—'earthlings', human beings, co-existing with a million other forms of life in the delicate ecology of this planet. In this continuing chain of giving and receiving, we live not only *with*, but *from* and *for* one another. The long history of gifts, the creative providence of God's acting on our behalf has led to the Word of God being present to us in person. The Word becomes flesh and dwells amongst us, to bring healing, forgiveness and abundant life. His cross reaches into the depths of the evil we suffer or cause, to promise reconciliation in an always greater love. His resurrection is our assurance that this long history of creative love will not be defeated. Love and life will have the last word, beyond anything we can imagine. The crowning gift of the Spirit is made to guide us into all truth, declaring 'the things that are to come' (Jn 16:13).

So much has been given to us, that we might exist and live. How, then, do we begin to repay what we owe in a non-inflationary currency? How do we too become a life-giving influence in return? How do we act in this economy of giving and grace?

7. Eucharistic Action

The Eucharistic command of the Lord, 'Do this in memory of me', arises from the imagination of one who gave himself without reserve for the sake of the many and the all. By entering into the spirit of Jesus' self-giving, we begin to have a heart open to all God's creation, refusing to leave out of our concerns any aspect of that good creation that the Creator has loved into being. By entering into Christ's imagination and becoming members of his body, we are in fact putting our souls back into our bodies. For we become

---

14. Toolan, 'Nature is an Heraclitean Fire', 43.

re-embodied in him who is related to everything and everyone. In and through him, we co-exist with all creation. We begin to live in a new time-frame determined by the patient, creative goodness of God who is working to draw all things to their fulfilment. We start to have time, beyond the pressures and compulsions of instant demand, to appreciate the wholeness of God's creation. We begin to own, as truly our own, what we had previously disowned or bypassed—above all, a living solidarity with the world of nature.

The Eucharist stimulates its own ecological perspectives. Everything has its part in God's creation. Everything has been owned by the divine Word in the incarnation. Everything is involved in the great transformation already begun in his resurrection. We are connected in a giving universe, at the heart of which is the self-giving love of God: 'Unless a grain of wheat falls into the earth and dies, it just a single grain; but if it dies, it bears much fruit' (Jn 12:24). We are living and dying into an ever larger selfhood. The true self is realised in a network of relationships within a communion pervading the whole of the universe. This self is shaped by the trinitarian relationships that constitute the very being of God.

The Eucharist, then, inspires us to welcome the great, generative reality of the cosmos and the ecological reality of our planetary biosphere in a more thankful spirit. The universe and this earth have their place in 'the Father's house of many dwelling places' (*cf* Jn 14:2).

To obey Jesus' command, 'Do this in memory of me', is to 're-member' all that has been dismembered in the sterile imagination of modern culture. The Eucharistic forms of faith, hope and love do not bypass either the universe or our planetary home. Spiritual progress is not an escape from what we are, but a generous reclamation of the world as destined for transformation. We cannot set nature aside, for it is our own flesh and blood. Loving our neighbour means loving the whole cosmic and planetary neighbourhood of our existence. In the measure we share the charged reality of the Eucharist, the Christian imagination expands to its fullest dimensions. Paul's prayer begins to be answered:

I pray that you may have the power to comprehend, with all the saints, what is the breadth and length and height and depth, and to know the love of Christ which surpasses knowledge, so that you may be filled with all the fullness of God (Eph 3:18–19).

The time and space of our earthly existence are filled with the energies of true life. Here and now, we are destined, not only to be jubilant participants in the feast but also, through all the giving and service that love demands, to be with Christ part of the meal. We contribute the energies of our lives to the great banquet of the new creation. With Jesus, we fall as grains of wheat into the holy ground to die, in order not to remain alone (Jn 12:24). Such a sense of life suggests a deeper understanding of nature and, indeed, of our earthly existence. The earth itself begins to appear, in the words of Beatrice Bruteau, as

> . . . the Eucharistic Planet, a Good Gift planet, which is structured in mutual feeding, as intimate self-sharing. It is a great Process, a circulation of living energies, in which the Real Presence of the Absolute is discerned.[15]

So it is the Eucharist envisions the world 'otherwise', that is, in its deepest and most hopeful reality. The sacrament of Christ's body and blood nourishes our minds and hearts into a sense of ecological wholeness. It cures the imagination of egotistical self-absorption to make it grow strong through a generous belonging to all. The need is expressed in the words of Einstein:

> A human being is part of the whole, called by us the 'universe', a part limited in time and space. He experiences himself, his thoughts and feelings, as something separated from the rest—a kind of optical delusion of his consciousness. This delusion is a kind of

---

15. Bruteau, 'Eucharistic Ecology and Ecological Spirituality', in *Cross Currents* (Winter 1990): 501.

prison for us, restricting us to our personal desires and to affection for a few persons nearest to us. Our task must be to free ourselves from this prison by widening our circle of compassion to embrace all living creatures and the whole of nature in its beauty.[16]

The relational existence that Christ nourishes inspires a sense of reality at odds with a self-enclosed individualistic vision. In expressing his Eucharistic relationship to us and our world, Jesus is acting out of his own sense of reality as field of communion and mutual indwelling. He prays, ' . . . that they may all be one. As you, Father, are in me and I in you, may they also be in us . . . I in them and you in me, that they may be completely one' (Jn 17:21–22). Our unity in God derives from the way the Father and the Son are united in the one divine life: the divine persons are not independent entities somehow managing to come together. Divine life is an eternal flow of one into the other, in relationships of mutual self-giving: 'Instead of taking as the norm of reality those things which are *outside* one another, he [Jesus] takes as a standard and paradigm those who are *in* one another.'[17] We are challenged to imagine our inter-relationships in terms of mutual indwelling modelled on the union existing between the Father and the Son. On this finite level, it is to nourish the other into being. And the life-giving nourishment we give is nothing less than the gift of ourselves. We are *in* one another for the life of the other. By being *from* the other, *for* the other, and so, *in* the other, our earthly-human lives participate in God's own trinitarian life and love.

The Eucharist inspires a deep ecological sensibility. Our ways of relating to everyone and everything in God's creation occur within a field of shared life and communion. The first movement of Christian existence is to give thanks (*eucharistia*) for the wonder of the love that has called us to be part of a commonwealth of life. Such

16. Albert Einstein, quoted in Michael Nagler, *America Without Violence* (Covelo, CA: Island Press,1982), 11.
17. Bruteau, 'Eucharistic Ecology. .', 502.

'thanking' deeply conditions the 'thinking' necessary to address the urgent ecological problems of our day. Obviously influenced by Eucharistic symbolism, a noted ecologist writes:

> To live, we must daily break the body and shed the blood of creation. When we do this knowingly, lovingly, skilfully, reverently, it is a sacrament. When we do it ignorantly, greedily, clumsily and destructively, it is desecration. In such a desecration, we condemn ourselves to spiritual, moral loneliness, and others to want.[18]

The Eucharist must affect, therefore, ecological integrity by providing the vision and the hope necessary to address the urgent problems now confronting the human race on planet Earth. A conscience formed by the Eucharist works against powerful cultural temptations to desecrate God's good creation. A sense of universal communion counteracts the spiritual and moral loneliness that threaten modern culture. The heartlessness that shuts out the poor and the needy from the great banquet of life is exposed to a redeeming influence. In all parts of the planet, in the daily round of millions of lives, the Eucharist is celebrated. The communities concerned awaken each day to a corporate rededication of themselves, not only to sharing the bread of life with the hungry, but also with a commitment to the ecological well-being of the planet itself. Faith awakens to the vision of the earth as a living sacrament of God's loving presence. As pilgrims, Christians move through time, but always walk on holy ground.

Conclusion

Some will feel that religious symbolism is one thing, while strategies of ecological action are quite another. Yet good action needs vision and imagination. Great symbols orientate us, body and soul,

---

18. Wendell Berry, *The Gift of Good Land* (North Point Press: San Francisco, 1981), 281.

individually and communally, within the living wholeness of reality, and give both the passion and patience to grapple with it. In this chapter we have reflected on the Eucharist as a primary symbol within the life of Christian faith. It is an essential expression of the poetry of such faith, unfolding as it does in a universe of grace. The Eucharistic vision radically re-shapes ecological experience, to make the unseen and the unspoken glow with significance, even if the struggle to find words for such matters remains. And yet there is a focus, for the Eucharist celebrates existence in the light of a Christ, the source and form of true life. We live indeed, by receiving what he gives, his body and blood. He breathes his Spirit into us and clothes us with his imagination: 'Do this in memory of me'. That means receiving him and even consuming the reality of his body and blood, but not in today's consumerist sense. For the gift remains undiminished, and makes those who receive it part of a new economy of giving, of communal life, and giving thanks. The Eucharist will always be the place to start again with new energy, hope and imagination, even in this critical time. The most direct and enduring of all biblical commandments continues in force, as the last words of the First Letter of John expresses it, 'Little children, keep yourselves from idols' (1 Jn 5:21).

It might seem that this dimension of integral ecology is only an eccentric mixture of metaphysics and mysticism, plus a little poetry, all leading to a sphere of exalted abstractions. On the other hand, a genuine ecological outlook must come down to earth, and keeps its feet on the ground. Not only ideas, but actions are necessary to for authentic ecological virtue. In this respect, the Eucharist is a radical way of acting. The *opus Dei* of the Eucharistic liturgy is not a matter of more thinking, nor a keener and more mystical manner of experiencing or living an exalted imagination. Nor, for that matter, is attention so concentrated on the nameless Other that a wide and deep experience of life in this world is excluded. In that regard the Eucharist is less about doing or producing something, but enacting the all-inclusive mystery in the time and space, in the midst of all the crises and contingencies affecting our common home. It celebrates the real sense of God in all creation, and, indeed, of all creation in

God. To that degree, Eucharistic action is at once an earthed and englobing activity. This is not to reduce the manifold reality of the world to a narrow band of religiosity, but of opening the pluriform reality of the world to both its real depth and its ultimate future. Performed in the here and now, the Eucharistic action is at once an affirmation and a hope: it means resisting the sheer oppressive weight of what is often called the 'secular' as opposed to the 'religious' while bring to expression an integral ecology of nature and grace. Liturgical action is an act of humility, patience, poverty of spirit and surrender to God in the world and in this earthly environment. In this respect, the Church is celebrating the Eucharist is that part of the world that enacts and brings to expression the universal mystery at work in all creation.

In this sense, liturgy is a refusal to allow the atmosphere of our common home to be suffocated by the spurious opposition of the religious and the secular, or the spiritual and the material. In the living environment, the secular and the material are too important to be divided and set at odds with the religious and the spiritual Such facets of creation appear within the horizon of God's creative action. The religious and the spiritual presume an explicit relationship to the living Source of creation, more really and actually than decorative additions to the rituals of a particular culture. In its daily or weekly round and through its yearly seasons, the Eucharistic liturgy 'does God' and all things in God, in the limitation and poverty of a moment in space and time. It means not holding to exalted moods, beautiful words, or noble sentiments, but being left with nothing but God, and with what God is doing in all creation as it anticipates its fulfilment in God. To that degree, liturgical activity is the expression of a radical poverty of spirit and cultural nakedness. Nonetheless, the Eucharistic liturgy, as the service of God, is world-forming, engendering a sense of wholeness and solidarity, in openness to the depths and heights of the present, and the eschatological future of God, all in all.[19]

---

19. Kevin Hart, 'Poverty's Speech: On Liturgical Reduction', in *Modern Theology* 31/4. (October 2015): 641–648.

The Eucharist, therefore, bears clear resemblances to all kinds of sacred rituals and their ways of offering participation in sacred space and sacred time. From a specifically Christian perspective, a number of particular features could be mentioned if the liturgy is to be presented as the activity of an integral ecology sensitive to the inspired scriptures, the real presence of Christ, the experience of grace, the communion of saints and so forth.

The confession of sins is a typical introductory rite in all Christian liturgical activities. It is a humble recognition of sinfulness when confronted with the reality of the evil we have caused or contributed to. The 'heart of flesh' of true thankfulness for the gifts of nature and grace thereby replaces the heart of stone that has wrought so much destructiveness. Any such transformation brought about by God cannot take place without an outpouring of mercy for the healing of our world and a new beginning. Confessing one's sins is neither a symptom of weakness or lack of integrity. The believer stands before God to acknowledge resistance to the will of God in thought word, deed and omission, that has resulted in poisoning creation and making the Creator less visible and credible in the world. The confession of sins is an intensely counter-cultural act—a movement into the God of creation, the ever-renewable source of blessing for all—and a recognition that the order of reality that is taken for granted in a consumerist culture is not as things should be.

Secondly, there is the liturgical focus on Christ. The readings from scripture place the sacramental celebration within the corporate history of Old and New Testaments. The Bible is not a compilation of information, but an invitation to enter through faith into the history of God's self-revelation in the world. Divine revelation continues as an ongoing and inexhaustible event, centered in the promise and fulfillment that have occurred in Christ. To that frame of mind, the Eucharist is celebrated within the horizon of the universe of God's creation in Christ. Consequently, the liturgy occurs in a God-charged field in which the universe—including this planetary biosphere, is being transformed into God's new creation, centred in Christ, 'the firstborn of all creation' (Col 1:15). Thus, the Eucharistic liturgy envisions, and even enacts, the world 'otherwise', as it is before God. Christ has occupied the depths and the heights of that world through his death and resurrection, culminating in ascension to the fullness of humanity with God. The liturgical doxology, 'through him, with him and in him' evokes the reality of the new creation in Christ as a field of communion and mutual indwelling. His disciples inhabit the world in a new way, as a community based in the unity the Father and the Son: 'that they may be one as we are one' (Jn 17:11). Jesus' ascent to the Father relocates believers into a space of holy communion and mutual indwelling: 'As you, Father, are in me, and I am in you, may they also be in us, so that the world may believe that you have sent me' (Jn 17:20–21).

By implication, the liturgical horizon unfolds in the inter-relationships and mutual indwelling deriving from the union existing between the Father and the Son. Each is *in* the other for the life of the other. By being from the other, for the other, and so, *in* the other, the liturgical praise of the Father, Son and Spirit arises from participation in God's own trinitarian life. This is to say that the Eucharist is not 'virtual reality' in any sense. It is a Spirit-inspired form of actual reality, communicating Christ as the 'real food' and 'real drink' of eternal life. In this regard, the liturgy of the Eucharist brings together what is often kept apart—the reality of God, consciousness of the self in relation to others, and the emerging universe itself. Centred on the 'real' presence of Christ, liturgical consciousness is not a distraction from the reality, but an immersion into it. The liturgy, therefore, 're-members' and brings together in a new integrity the fractured experience of humanity and its world. As holy communion, it joins believers to Christ's Body, and summons them to participate in its growth. The risen and ascended Christ, he is not *here* in any sense of worldly location, but present beyond any worldly measure or containment. Christ is not located in the world because that world now exists in him (Col 1:16).

Liturgical experience is not shaped as a compensation for Christ absent from the world, but as related to that world in a new way.

Humanity has not been discarded in the risen and ascended Christ. Heaven, in Christian terms, therefore is not a vague celestial and unreal location, but communion with God in Christ in a creation transformed. As a result, humanity and the created universe find a new integrity. The liturgy enacts the manner in which, in Christ, the world has been irreversibly ascended into the life of God, and God descended into the life of the world. The liturgy is, therefore, not an imaginative attempt to fit Christ into an unredeemed world, but rather a celebration of how the world and the entire creation are contained and embodied in him. Christ is the milieu and environment of creation already made new, in anticipation of what is still to be realised fully.

6

Integral Ecology and *Sister Death*

Pope Francis has no romantic view of the world, given his robust denunciation of consumerism, his sensitivity to the sufferings of the earth and its people, his lamentation over the disappearance of so many species of fauna and flora, and his special reference to the deaths of the poor and infants [20, 20, 48].[1] All these are evidences of a sober realism. Nonetheless, there is little mention of death in *Laudato Si': On the Care for Our Common Home*. Nor does he include in his citation of the Canticle of St Francis the verse the saint added as his own death approached, 'Be praised my Lord through our Sister Bodily Death, from whose embrace no living person can escape'. In the interests of a genuine integral ecology, therefore, this chapter considers the ecological and theological significance of death and how it affects and inspires 'care for our common home'.

Before moving to a consideration of 'Sister Death', a familiar presence in the life of this planet, we will pause over what we mean by an 'integral ecology', above all in *Laudato Si'*.[2] Negatively, an integral ecology is opposed to the two extremes, either that of reducing ecological methods to purely empirical procedures and technocratic controls; or to, say, a green spirituality that disdains

---

1. Numbers in square brackets correspond to the numbered paragraphs in *Laudato Si'*.
2. There are many references to 'integral' describing development, education and ecology in *Laudato Si'*, see especially paragraphs 10, 11, 62, 124, the whole of Chapter 4, 137, 141,147, 159, 197, 225, 230. The phrase, 'integral ecology' first appears in a 2009 document of the International Theological Commission which recognises the need for the Catholic 'natural law' tradition to be open to ecological perspectives—and for these to recognise a fundamental natural law. See, 'In search of universal ethic: A New Look at Natural Law', paragraph 82.

the findings of science. More positively, an integral outlook will presume an appreciation of the planetary environment, and show a capacity to diagnose how it has been harmed by uncaring exploitation. But this must be correlated to the 'inner ecology' of culture. Without a conversion of mind and heart, in a both a personal and social sense, there can be little hope for any turn-around in our relationship to world of nature and the delicate interrelationships and synergies it discloses. Further, without a shareable discourse on basic human values, the prospects of considering the common good or the integrity of the environment diminish. An integral ecology, therefore, must insist that the fact and mystery of death in the interdisciplinary collaborative framework it envisages. That will mean leaving unanswered questions that cannot be answered, and deferring to hope in Christ crucified and risen for a deeper appreciation of 'sister death' in the universe of God's creation.[3]

As this chapter progresses and examines various sensibilities and theoretical understandings regarding death, certain questions keep recurring as each position is outlined, such as how this particular approach to death affects an integral ecology of our planetary environment and its responsibility for 'our common home'. By reflecting on death in an ecological context, we can ensure that the framework of integral ecology will remain open, and radically undecided, unless the witness of Christian faith and hope is invoked. In this way, faith in Christ is an ever renewable resource in a world of dwindling resources.

But that is to run ahead when efforts to name the reality of death tend to oscillate between two classic statements. The first expresses an immemorial sense of tragedy of death: *Sunt lacrimae rerum et mentem mortalia tangunt* [4] (translatable as, 'there are tears at the heart of things, and all mortal things affect the mind'). Such words can only intensify the widespread lament over the environmental destruction that has been wrought on the life of the planet, so often

---

3.   For an informed and inspiring account, see Denis Edwards, *Ecology at the Heart of Faith* (Maryknoll, NY: Orbis, 2006).
4.   Virgil, *Aeneid*, I, 462.

by human agencies. The other is the statement of the Johannine Jesus: 'Unless the grain of wheat falls into the earth and dies, it remains just a single grain; but if it dies, it bears much fruit' (Jn 12:24). Here, too, there is an inevitable sense of diminishment, but it is taken up into the ultimate hope for transformation and communion. The implication is that death and dying have an essential place in life and serve the purposes of the 'sublime communion' [89] that God is bringing about. Admittedly, the fact and reality of death permit no theoretical synthesis of the psychological, philosophical, theological and ecological actors involved.[5] Nonetheless, the five headings under which this chapter will be presented, will, we hope, serve to deepen reflection and sharpen conscience.

1. The Deadliness of Death
2. The Denial of Death
3. Death in Christ
4. Before the Foundation of the World
5. The Realm of Otherness

1. The Deadliness of Death

While Paul declares that 'living is Christ, and dying his gain' (Phil 1:21), his words describe the hope of one who have arrived at the summit of Christian faith. On the other hand, the brute fact of death is a universal and intrusive reality, especially when it occurs in its most violent and alien form. Death figures in our cultural perceptions in two major ways. First, there is what might be regarded as a 'cooler' view. Death is a matter-of-fact biological reality. Indeed, it is a necessary feature inscribed into the dynamics

---

5. Lucy Bregman, *Death, Dying, Spirituality and Religions. A Study of the Death Awareness Movement* (New York: Peter Lang, 2003) presents a many-faceted movement approaching the phenomenon of death as a meaningful experience beyond the specifically medical context. Her interdisciplinary movement can appear to be purely secular, but, in fact, it tends to draw on the spirituality latent in classic and popular expressions of Judaism, Christianity and Buddhism—and more besides.

of evolution. There can be no progress in the evolutionary scheme of things unless death ensures the succession of generations. It is the price to be paid for the evolution of life on earth. It makes possible the emergence of differentiated, complex living beings in a world of wonderful bio-diversity. Unless we belong to the mortal world of life on this planet, human beings would never have come into existence.[6]

Moreover, there is a sober, scientific backdrop to individual death. It is the eventual collapse of the solar system, even if billions of years from now. And that will entail the extinction of all life on this planet. Of more dramatic menace is the most probable reoccurrence of cosmic events that have been lethal to planetary life in the past. William R Stoeger, SJ, in his scientific account of catastrophes in this life-bearing universe, considers matters within a time-frame of fifty million years – enough time for the appearance and disappearance of a species. He writes:

> The prime reason for discussing [such possibilities] . . . is though they are remote and of long-time-scale occurrence, they are certain to happen. They also represent the ultimate demise of life on this planet, and, in the case of the universe, of the cosmic life-bearing womb itself. As such, they represent a very formidable challenge to our religious understanding of what ultimate destiny, eternal life, the resurrection of the body, and the new heavens and the new earth might mean.[7]

In other words, 'the mystery of life and death are written into the very heart and essence of material creation'.[8] The law of entropy is built

6. Denis Edwards, *Breath of Life. A Theology of the Creator Spirit* (Maryknoll, NY: Orbis, 2004), 137–138; 174.

7. William R Stoeger, SJ, 'Scientific Accounts of Ultimate Catastrophes in our Life-Bearing Universe', in *The End of the World and the Ends of God*, edited by J Polkinghorne and M Welker (19-28), 21.

8. Stoeger, 'Scientific Accounts', 28.

into the cosmos itself. All systems break down; and the fundamental chaos which they order and control finally takes over. This point of view is characterized by a dispassionate scientific objectivity. An integral ecology is made to include a range of scientific data on the inevitable death of the universe. On the other hand, this outlook serves to highlight the wonder of life and all the varied life-forms that have appeared—in their improbable contingency. To this degree, *data* begin to appear as *dona*, and call forth gratitude to a giver for the gift of sheer existence.

There is a 'hot' version of death as well. The earth has lived under the threat of megadeath for decades. Though human history has always known its catalogue of natural disasters, famines, earthquakes, plagues—'acts of God'—we now live with the eerie possibility of death-dealing human activities affecting the planet. Biological warfare, thermonuclear incineration, and ecological destruction still menace life on this planet. Huge technological systems shape the ecological, social, political and economic world. The consumerist economy is insatiable in its demands. Enormous military arsenals at the disposition of dozens of governments openly include weapons of mass destruction designed for biological or thermonuclear warfare. This range of lethal capacities is the material expression of a readiness to wipe out whole populations if the necessity arises. Given that the possibilities of 'heat death' are taken for granted in the contemporary environment, the task of an integral ecology is clarified, namely, to mitigate the probabilities of global self-destruction—so to work for the disarmament of the heart, and the kind of reconciliation that can remove environmental threats from our common home.

2. The Denial of Death

After noting factual approaches to the inevitability of death, we now move on to more subjective considerations associated with the denial of such a reality.

The dread of death goes some way in explaining morbid aspects of modern culture such as obsessive consumerism, deracinated individualism and careless destruction of the environment. As Ernest Becker expresses the thesis of his now classic work, *The Denial of Death*:

> The idea of death, the fear of it, haunts the human animal like nothing else; it is the mainspring of human activity—activity designed largely to avoid the fatality of death, to overcome it by denying in some way that it is the final destiny for man.[9]

Though Becker acknowledges the enormous influence of Freud in the understanding of psychopathology, he is also critical. For Becker, the fundamental repression or denial in human life is not related to the sexual, as Freud had taught, but to death. Hence, the purpose of therapy is to free the suffering person to live with the most radical fear of all, which has its origin in our common mortality. But what, then, are human beings to do with the fact that they and the natural world they inhabit are all inevitably on the way to death.

Melancholic though such a question might sound, it poses deeper questions about the urgent ecological matters and their larger cosmic connections. Becker insists that we face the primordial terror that affects the human psyche in the face of death, and this means accepting a radical acceptance of creaturehood. As creatures, we are immersed in the wholeness of nature, connected to it, caught up and carried along by it. The paradox is that, only by accepting our limitation and contingency within a larger whole, only by yielding ourselves into the life-process, this stream of life and death, can we arrive at true freedom and psychic health.

Religious experience, Becker argues, is essentially a 'creature feeling' in the face of the massive transcendence of creation. In this respect, the human is a tiny, vulnerable instance of existence within the overwhelming miracle of the universe. At this juncture, 'religion and psychology find a talking point—right at the point of

---

9.　Ernest Becker, *The Denial of Death* (New York: The Free Press, 1973), ix.

the problem of courage'.[10] Faced with the immensity of the universe and its apparent impassivity in regard to individual fate:

> man had to invent and create out of himself the limitations of perception and equanimity to live on this planet. And so the core of psychodynamics, the formation of the human character, is a study in human self-limitation and in the terrifying costs of that limitation. [11]

There will be a predictable hostile reaction to facing up to 'the terrifying costs' of recognising reality. In not wanting to accept the limits of life on this planet, we begin to live a lie about ourselves and the world we inhabit. Indeed, Becker speaks of human character as a 'vital lie', based in denial, illusion and pretence.[12]

Ecological and cosmological perspectives can either expose this 'vital lie' of culture, or, by denying death in their respective ways, feed it with further self-deception. On the other hand, facing the reality of death leads to a deeper, more wonderful participation in the mystery of life. For genuine authenticity can be realised only through the courageous acceptance of creatureliness. In a more philosophical and religious range of reference, Becker writes: 'By being or doing, we fashion something, an object or ourselves, and drop it into the confusion, make an offering of it, so to speak, to the life-force.'[13] He is calling us, in effect, to a lived sense of relationality, and to the virtues of praise and thankfulness that are at the heart of religious faith. Yet a shared sense of the human condition promises renewed collaboration between science and religion. Science improperly absorbs all truth into itself while the role of religion to stand for a larger version of truth. For its part, religious faith enables human beings,

---

10. Becker, *The Denial*, 50.
11. Becker, *The Denial*, 51.
12. Becker, *The Denial*, 51.
13. Becker, *The Denial*, 285.

> To wait in a condition of openness toward miracle and
> mystery, in the lived truth of creation, which would
> make it easier to survive and be redeemed because men
> would be less driven to undo themselves and would
> be more like the image which pleases their creator:
> awe-filled creatures trying to live in harmony with the
> rest of creation. Today we would add . . . they would be
> less likely to poison the rest of creation.[14]

Faith, then, has a contemplative dimension in its reverent openness
to the mystery of creation and the Creator. Likewise, it exercises a
redemptive effect in causing human beings to be less driven to self-
destruct, and more disposed to realise the divine image in the works
of love and justice. More to the point, the religious sense of the
Creator and creation is of ecological value in that it demands living
in harmony with 'the rest of creation', and lessens the likelihood
of poisoning it. Most of all, a genuinely creaturely consciousness
relativises the harmful effects of the 'denial of death'. To accept our
puniness in the face of the overwhelming majesty of the universe,
to become aware of the unspeakable miracle of even a single living
being, and so, begin to waken to the chaotic depths of the immense,
inconclusive drama of creation. This is to come to a point of healing.

Following Frederick Perls, Becker detects four protective layers
structuring the neurotic, death-denying self. The first two layers are
the mundane, everyday layers of cliché and role which affect most
our lives and provide the criterion of success measured in terms of
the right image. It is undoubtedly a considerable achievement to
break out of image of the self as it is imposed and communicated
by an individualistic and consumerist culture. But Becker points to
more resistant and armoured areas of the self, what the rhetoric of
the spiritual life would describe as the darkness of the intellect and
the hardness of heart of those resisting grace :

> . . . . the third is the stiff one to penetrate: it is the impasse
> that covers our feelings of being empty and lost, the very

---

14. Becker, *The Denial*, 282.

feeling we try to banish in building up our character
defences. Under this layer is the fourth and the most
baffling one: the 'death' or fear-of-death layer; this . . .
is the layer of our true and basic animal anxieties, the
terror that we carry around in our secret heart. Only
when we explode this fourth layer . . . do we get to the
layer of what we might call our 'authentic self': what
we really are without shame, without disguise, without
defences against fear.[15]

The authentic self, therefore, is realised in connectedness and
harmony with all creation. It might be fittingly termed the 'ecological'
or 'cosmic' self—that is, the *religious* self as described above, bonded
to the Creator and all creation—in contrast to the tiny scope of the
fear-driven illusory self produced by the denial of death. In effect,
the true self is realised only by befriending the mortal character of
existence.

As a consequence, authenticity consists in regaining the attitude
of humility, a sense of radical finiteness proper to creatureliness.[16]
The great value of Becker's work for an ecological and Christian
spirituality lies in its revaluation of humility, in the most original
sense of the word. 'Humility', from the Latin *humus*, meaning earth,
soil, dirt. It indicates an awareness of the existential fact that spiritual
life is earthed, grounded, bound up with immense dynamism of
nature into whose processes we are each and all immersed. Hence,
the ancient liturgical injunction on Ash Wednesday, as the ashes are
traced on the forehead in the sign of the Cross: *Memento homo quia
pulvus es. . .*: 'Remember, man, thou art but dust . . .' In the catalogue
of moral virtues, humility is a quality of freedom. It is shown in a
radical decentring of the self, in the recognition that all is given,
and that existence is a gift. In this respect, humility enables human
consciousness to deal honestly creatively with the dread of death by

---

15. Becker, *The Denial*, 57.
16. Becker, *The Denial*, 58. See also Andras Angyal, *Neurosis and Treatment: a Holistic
    Theory* (New York: Wiley, 1965), 260.

recognising oneself as a creature within the mystery of the vast and uncanny universe.

Thus, death is allowed to emerge from its subterranean place of influence, no longer to sap our energies or drive us to the frenzy of illusory immortality-projects. Humility is a connective virtue, relating us to the whole, and immersing each and all in a wondrous universe of gifts and giving. If ecological virtue is to be more than posturing, the cultivation of humility as a basic attitude in regard to life and creation is an obvious imperative. For out of this humble acceptance of mortality can come the wisdom we need if we are to coexist on this planet as 'our common home'. Life remains a question, within an overwhelmingly uncanny universe. It is most clear that that none of us is the centre of that universe, for we have emerged out of a vast cosmic process, and are dying back into it. When we begin to ask about the true centre, the true life-force of this overwhelming universe, an acceptance of self as mortal and finite begins. With that, if not precisely adoration, at least surrender to the often unnamed, incomprehensible creative generosity at the origin of all being and life can be realised. Only a de-centred self, conscious of its mortal limitation, can live from and for a larger mystery, and in an integral ecology.

Becker's phenomenology of the psychology of fear and denial deserves recognition in an integral ecology. He notably stresses the existential value of the moral virtue of humility in our human sense of the universe, along with value of what we might call a 'kenotic' attitude of self-surrender in life and in death. To this degree, his approach is powerfully religious, and anticipates what we present below as 'death in Christ'. In the present context, the manner in which Becker connects befriending death with living in harmony with all creation, while 'the denial of death' can lead to the poisoning of the environment.

Becker's reflection resembles the biblical connection of death to sin as a punishment. Death is shrouded in a darkness deeper than the inevitable termination of biological life. Death, Paul declares, is the 'wages of sin' (Rom 6:23). The implication is that death is the consequence and manifestation of sin. Sin is basically alienation from God, and the refusal of communion with the Creator—and creation. It is the choice for one's self against all others. In this context, the seemingly natural fact of death becomes the carrier of a profound sense of rupture and guilt. It looms through life as 'the last enemy' (1 Cor 15:26).[17]

Human culture is infected with the bias of 'original sin'.[18] We are born into a world skewed away from its centre and disrupted in the communion that God intends. To the degree existence is self-centred, death is experienced as menacing and meaningless. Life and death are locked in an absurd conflict, with death assured of victory. The transcendent Otherness of God and the created otherness of our neighbour cannot but appear as a threat. Everything is subjected to the self-serving demands of a skewed human freedom. The more human existence is turned in on itself, the more it occupies a shrinking universe. As a result, human identity is formed in competitive self-assertion against the Other. In this respect, death is the deepest threat: 'The wages of sin is death'. Death holds no promise of life; it is the carrier of all that is meaningless and threatening to the life we have chosen and made.[19]

The idea of death as the wages of sin invites an application to environmental issues. Environmental destruction brought about by human greed and carelessness regarding the loss of biodiversity, to say nothing of their lethal effect on the lives of the poor amounts to a planetary instance of what the sins of pride greed and selfishness can lead to. As the next section, 'Death in Christ', will indicate, death experienced as the wages of sin invite a deeper appreciation of the death of Christ and of Christian participation in his death and resurrection. Even aside from conversion to Christ, illusions born of the denial of death cannot be total. Life contests the reign of death as total, for in ordinary lives know sudden impulses of wonder, unnameable hope and the exhilaration of great loves, just as

---

17. James Alison, *The Joy of Being Wrong. Original Sin Through Easter Eyes* (New York: Crossroad, 1998) is illuminating in this whole area.
18. Alison, *The Joy of Being Wrong*, is a basic reference.
19. Karl Rahner, *On the Theology of Death*, translated by CH Henkey (New York: Herder & Herder, 1962). 32-51.

all are humbled before the strange grandeur of moral achievement. In such moments, there is an uncanny, death resistant, "more" in the experience of the mystic, the artist, the martyr, the prophet, the thinker, the scientist and the activist. There is an intimation of eternity in the making, of 'eternity coming to be as time's own mature fruit'.[20]

Here a brief comparison of Becker's *Denial of Death* with Boros' *Mysterium Mortis*[21] is useful. Located in a classical philosophical and spiritual tradition, Boros' approach takes up where Becker's ends. He concedes that, empirically speaking, death implies dissolution and destruction. But Boros is intent on asking, 'whether the complete removal from self which we undergo in death does not conceal a much more fundamental process which could be described . . . in terms of the progressive achievement of selfhood, of actively initiating the self to life'.[22] Like Becker, Boros purports to be exploring human consciousness. But instead of highlighting the strategies involved in the denial of death, Boros seeks to illumine the dynamics of self-transcendence discernible in actual living. A positive hermeneutics of mortality suggests that the thrust of human life is toward fulfillment—*in*, and even *through*, death. In dying, an individual existence moves to the bounds of its being. It awakes to a kind of full knowledge and liberty. The dynamics of personal existence that moved and motivated life in its normal course have been largely hidden from consciousness. At the moment of death, however, these surface into full awareness. Our deepest being is revealed as 'of unimaginable splendor', as the full dimensions of our being unfold.[23] In this respect, the self dies out of the limited individuality of the ego, into a more deeply relational form of being. This is to become aware of oneself as part of the universal whole, a new form of consciousness registering,

---

20. See Peter C Phan, *Eternity in Time: A Study of Karl Rahner's Eschatology* (London: Associated University Press, 1988), 55. Also, 53–58; 207–210.
21. Ladislaus Boros, *The Moment of Truth: Mysterium Mortis*, translated by G Bainbridge (London: Burns and Oates, 1962).
22. Boros, *The Moment of Truth*, viii. For elaboration, 1–23.
23. Boros, *The Moment of Truth*, viii. See 73–81.

> . . . all at once and all together the universe that
> [the human person] has always borne hidden
> within himself, the universe with which he is
> already most intimately united, and which, one
> way or another, was always being produced from
> within him.[24]

The horizon in which this totality is experienced at the limits of
our existence is now bounded only by the infinite mystery of God:
'Being flows toward [the person in death] like a boundless stream
of things, meanings, persons and happenings, ready to convey him
right into the Godhead.'[25] Death, therefore, is meeting with God. This
limitless Other has been present in every stirring of our existence. It
has been within us as our 'deepest mystery'. It has worked within all
the elements and causes that have formed us, moving us towards an
eternal destiny.[26] In the light of God, we are brought to a moment
of final decision:

> There now man stands, free to accept or reject this
> splendor. In a last final decision, he either allows this
> flood of realities to flow past him, while he stands there
> eternally turned to stone, like a rock past which the
> life-giving stream flows on, noble enough in himself no
> doubt, but abandoned and eternally alone; or he allows
> himself to be carried along by this flood, becomes part
> of it and flows on to eternal fulfilment.[27]

Thus, Boros dramatically evokes the moment of decision when
death occurs is the final opportunity to crystallize one's life in a
completely personal act. Paradoxically, it is our most fully conscious
and free moment. It faces us with the decision—to choose life and
the God of life for whom we were made. Where Becker takes us

---

24. Boros, *The Moment of Truth*.
25. Boros, *The Moment of Truth*.
26. Boros, *The Moment of Truth*, ix.
27. Boros, *The Moment of Truth*, ix, and elaborated in 73–84.

back to the psyche's primordial terror in the face of mortality, Boros bids us yield to the movement of the human spirit anticipating its final homecoming. All in all, art, mysticism, love and intelligence are promises that are yet to be kept. In death, the self-transcending movement of our existence will find its ultimate point of rest and its final vindication.[28]

As regards the concerns of this chapter, It would do violence to history and to the achievement of writer of great influence sixty years ago, to expect any ecological application of his presentation of the *mysterium mortis*. His concern is clearly the eschatological realisation of the self in the presence of God, and he does not deal with how such a hope would affect the understanding if integral ecology in the present. In this respect, Boros' brilliant analysis of the meaning of death is not incompatible with Becker's sense of creaturehood and creation. Nonetheless, he does tend to give the impression that in death the human spirit escapes this present world for the sake of an eschatological fulfilment somewhat isolated from the universe of God's creation of all things in Christ.

Each of the approaches of Becker and Boros we have summarily sketched appeal to reasonably accessible levels of human experience. Where Becker points to the repressed depths of consciousness, Boron points to its heights. The one uncovers a primitive terror in the face of death. The other presents the thrust of life as somehow positing death as the door to a final self-realisation. Psychologically speaking, Becker's approach is more archeological. It searches into the psychic terror that affects culture with a 'denial of death'. Boros is more teleological in that it elucidates the movement of human existence in a manner best described as an affirmation or vindication of self-transcending consciousness.

At this point, we touch on a complex problem: How can hope find a psychological focus that is neither depressive nor schizophrenic? If it is morbid to constrict the whole hopeful direction of life to inevitable death, it would be just as evasive to repress the piercing tragedy at the heart of our existence. Facing death demands that

28. See Phan, *Eternity in Time*, 75–115.

we hold together both the negative and the positive dimensions of experience, even though these extremes never simply meet in any overall synthesis, even in an integral ecology. Here, the death of Christ, crucified and risen, recalls us to refocus our reflections on what faith reveals.

3. Death in Christ

Jacques Derrida's *The Gift of Death*[29] confronts his readers with the question of death, in a context formed by a number of major European thinkers, for example, Kierkegaard, Heidegger, Lévinas. He focuses on a writer little known in the English-speaking world, the Czech philosopher, Jan Patocka.[30] With Vaclev Havel, he authored *Charta 77* on human rights, and died of a brain haemorrhage after eleven hours of interrogation by the Czechoslovakian police during the Communist regime in 1977. For Patocka, the meaning of death was not only of deeply personal significance but also radically affected European culture and history. At the heart of that history, there is an abyss always resisting any totalising, theoretical solution or any reduction of human fate to the economy of exchange or reward. The dizzying excess of factual scientific knowledge characteristic of the West conceals the fact that there is no ever-ready answer to this question, unless it be given—right into the 'black hole' of death itself. The task of historical responsibility is to be open to the possibility of such a gift which can be received only in faith. Authenticity at this point means a readiness to venture, beyond any knowledge or security, into absolute risk, so to enter into relationship with the transcendent Other, the God of selfless goodness, offered as a gift even in death itself.

In that venture, at that point of conversion, a new self is disclosed as the recipient of the gift, within the abyss in which history finds itself. True freedom is realised only in the waiting. Patocka observes,

---

29. Jacques Derrida, *The Gift of Death*, translated by David Wills (Chicago: The University of Chicago Press, 1995).
30. See Erazim Kohak, *Jan Patocka: Philosophy and Selected Writings* (Chicago: University of Chicago Press, 1989); and Jan Patocka, *Heretical Essays on the Philosophy of History* (Chicago: Open Court Publishing, 1995).

> In the final analysis, the soul is not in relationship to an object, however elevated, such as the Platonic Good . . . which governs the ideal order of the Greek *polis* of the Roman *civitas*, but to a person who fixes it in his gaze while at the same time remaining beyond the reach of the gaze of the soul. As for knowing what that person is, such a question has not yet received an adequate thematic development within the perspective of Christianity.[31]

What, then, has theology been doing? In the risk of his own life, Patocka felt both an unsurpassable hope and a certain failure in Christian thought regarding the expression of the gift and the transcendent giver:

> Because of its foundation within the abyssal profundity of the soul, Christianity represents to this day the most powerful means—n ever yet superseded but not yet thought right through either—by which man is able to struggle against his own decline.[32]

Patocka's vision into the abyss in both history and the human spirit can provoke further reflection in today's experience of the destruction of the planetary environment and the ecological crisis that has ensued. Even here, we wait with him in this experience of death, for the gift to continue be given in a consciousness transformed by Christian hope. Inspiring that transformation, there is an event which can allow both hope and failure to co-exist and illumine each another, namely, the crucifixion and death of Christ himself.[33] Christian meditation is not fixated on a skull, but on the cross of Jesus—which, in deepest meaning, it is a theophany. The all-creative

---

31. As quoted in Derrida, *The Gift of Death*, 25.
32. Derrida, *The Gift of Death*, 28.
33. Gustave Martelet, *L'au-delà retrouvé. Christologie des fins dernières* (Paris: Desclée, 1975), 33–98.

mystery reveals itself through the cross as compassionate and transforming love. The death of Jesus was indeed deadly. It occurred as failure, betrayal isolation, condemnation, torture and execution. God's love felt the force of the human problem of evil. However, the love that gave itself to the end (Jn 13:1) was not defeated by the power of evil.[34] For the death of the crucified Jesus enacts and embodies the ultimate form of life as he surrenders himself to the Father in solidarity with the defeated and the lost. With his existence is concentrated in a final point of self-offering, God is self-revealed as a love stronger than death, as the creative mystery that upholds and fulfils all the best energies of life. To that degree, the crucified and risen One is the 'white hole' in the world of death. In Christ, crucified and risen, those receptive to the divine Gift are summoned to pass over from a self-serving existence into the realm of eternal life, already begun in the faith, hope and love, the gifts that will last (1 Cor 13:13). Death, too, remains as the limit of this form of earthly life, but now transformed into an act of ultimate surrender to the Father in union with Christ, in yielding to the creativity of the Spirit who makes all things new. What is implied in death so understood is a participation in a larger vitality, and communion in an ultimate co-existence. The dissolution of death means rising to a new level of being, in the radiant space of Jesus' resurrection.[35] The entropy affecting each individual biological existence is dissipated to allow for a higher realisation of communion, in relationship to the 'all' and participation in the whole.

The vector of self-transcendence in the direction of communion is underwritten, as it were, in the dynamics of the cosmos itself. The sense of self as a self-contained particle is revealed to be the wave of communion, the relational self. There is an upward vector of ascent from electron, to atoms, to molecules, to proteins, to cells, to organisms, to the complexity of the human brain, and to the cosmic

---

34. See Anthony J Kelly and Francis F Moloney, *Experiencing God in the Gospel of John* (New York: Paulist Press, 2003), 270–286.

35. Denis Edwards, 'Resurrection and the Costs of Evolution: A Dialogue with Rahner on Non-Interventionist Theology', in *Theological Studies* 67 (2006): 816–833—especially 827–833.

overture of human consciousness. The direction of life is one of transformation in increasingly rich and complex relationships. Might not the notion of death be more hopefully and realistically located in such a process? In that context, death would not mean dissolution so much as the expansion of the self into its fullest relationality. Death would not be an alien intruder, but a relative— 'Sister Death' as St Francis could pray—within cosmic promise of the fullness of life in Christ.

It is true that the resurrection is not resuscitation to this present biological life, nor does it entail a relocation in the time and space of this world. It is no cure for death. Only a transformation of our whole embodied existence can answer the hopes written into life. By participating in his rising from the tomb, the entropy and limiting individuality of biological life, is definitively overcome. In him a new creation is anticipated when Christ is given as 'the resurrection and the life' (Jn 11:25). The particular realism of this new creation is expressed in all four Gospel narratives in regard to the empty tomb. It the historical marker of the cosmic transformation that has begun in Christ:[36] 'So if anyone is in Christ, there is a new creation: everything old has passed away; see, everything has become new!' (2 Cor 5:17).

Hope, nonetheless remains hope. It lives always in the in-between of what is, and what is yet to be, as it waits on the mystery of final transformation. Even the New Testament writer soberly concedes, 'As it is, we do not yet see everything in subjection to him' (Heb 2: 8f). Yet for all the sobriety of Christian hope, the great conviction is remains firm. In Christ, the universe has been changed. Death has been radically 'Christened'. Christ did not die out of the world, but into it, to become its innermost coherence and dynamism. Indeed, in his death, resurrection and ascension, the mystery of the incarnation is complete. For the Christian, dying in Christ is to surrender to the transforming power of such a resurrection, so to be newly embodied in the future form of cosmos itself:[37]

---

36. On the empty tomb, see Anthony J Kelly, *The Resurrection Effect: Transforming Christian Life and Thought* (Maryknoll NY: Orbis, 2008), 139–145.

37. For elaboration of this point, see Denis Edwards, *Jesus and the Cosmos* (New York: Paulist Press, 1991), 103–132.

> The last enemy to be destroyed is death . . . When all
> things are subjected to him, the Son himself will also
> be subjected to him who put all things under him, that
> God may be all in all (1 Cor 15:26–28).

All mortal existence is poised, therefore, over an abyss of life. The empty tomb, a sign of the creative power of the Spirit, is of cosmic significance.[38] It suggests the full-bodied reality of resurrection, and seeds history with questions and wonder as to what great transformation is afoot. The empty tomb, so soberly recorded in each of the four Gospels, offers no salvation in mere emptiness. It functions as a factor within the awakening of faith, as a new consciousness of life unfolds. It moves first from the empty tomb, discovered as a puzzling fact. It awakens to cosmic surprise over what had happened, for Jesus appears as newly and wonderfully alive: 'Do not be afraid. I am the first and the last, and the living one. I was dead, and see, I am alive forever and ever' (Rev 1:17–18). Then faith returns to the tomb as an emblem of the new creation. From there it expands into the limitless horizons of a transformation of all things in Christ. Such faith is not primarily looking back at a death, but facing forward into the promise of eternal life, in a universe transformed.

4. Before the Foundation of the World

In the meantime we are confronted with the agony of the world and the cost of evolution, with its deaths, extinctions, violence and dead ends: 'the whole of creation has been has been groaning in labor pains until now' (Rom 8:23). Note, for instance, the extinction of the eighty thousand extraordinarily complex creatures of the Cambrian period, unearthed in the Burgess Shale in British Columbia.[39] Side-

---

38. John Polkinghorne, *Science and Creation. The Search for Understanding* (London: SPCK, 1988), 64–68.
39. For an abundance of documentation and marvellous instances of fossil remains, see Stephen Jay Goulding, *Wonderful Life: The Burgess Shale and the Nature of History* (London: Penguin, 1989).

by-side with the cosmic cooperation that enables the evolutionary process, 'competition, pain, and death (are) intrinsic to evolutionary processes'.[40] In the agony and struggle inscribed in nature itself, we turn to the image of 'the Lamb that was slaughtered before the foundation of the world' (Rev 13:8; see also Rev 5:6, 11–12; 7:13–17; 12:11). This image suggests that there is an aboriginally self-giving divine love constitutive of the creation and providence. Without such a perspective, human and evolutionary history could lead to a blank wall of hopelessness. The self-giving love of God constitutive of creation is expressed in several places in the New Testament. Paul affirms that Christ Jesus emptied himself of 'the form of God', to take on the form of a slave (Phil 2:5–7).[41] In post-Pauline developments, the author of the Letter to the Colossians describes the Christ as 'the image of the invisible God, the first born of all creation . . . He himself is before all things, and in him all things hold together' (Col 1:15, 17). Similarly, the Letter to the Ephesians proclaims: 'He chose us in him before the foundation of the world to be holy and blameless before him in love' (Eph 1:4). Then, at the foundation of Johannine Christology is the intimate union between the *Logos* with God that pre-existed 'the beginning' (Jn 1:1–2). In his final prayer, the Johannine Jesus prays to his Father that he might return to the glory which was his in God's presence 'before the world existed' (Jn 17:5).[42]

Completing and intensifying this perspective of God's original, preexistent and sacrificial love, is the vision of the slaughtered and risen lamb shining into all the darkness and violence of history, 'from the foundation of the world' (Rev 5:6; 13:8). This light must be taken to penetrate even into the evolutionary *agōnia* of the cosmos,[43] for

---

40. Denis Edwards, *Partaking of God: Trinity, Evolution and Ecology* (Collegeville, MN: Liturgical Press), 88; further, 130–46, where Edwards discusses 'Evolution, Cooperation, and the Theology of Original Sin'.

41. For a convincing exegetical and theological argument in favour of pre-existence, see Brendan Byrne, 'Christ's Pre-Existence in Pauline Soteriology', in *Theological Studies*, 58 (1997): 308–30.

42. The incarnate *Logos*, known as 'Jesus Christ' (Jn 1:14-17), is the key to the mystery of the Johannine Jesus.

43. Revelation's presentation of the sheer grace of Jesus' death and resurrection 'from

suffering and death are a necessary part of the evolutionary process.[44] The realism of faith in the Crucified cannot hide from the agony of the Cross; nor fail to relate it to the suffering and dying inherent in an evolutionary universe within this planetary environment. The author of Revelation locates Jesus' sacrifice for the sins of the world as primordial, as 'before the foundation of the world'. That is to suggest that the failures and ambiguities of creation that have occurred from the beginnings of time can be already washed clean by the blood of the Lamb (Rev 7:13–17). The key element in the relationship of God to the world, that is—from 'before the foundation of the world'—has been the continuing presence of the crucified and risen One: 'Do not be afraid; I am the first and the last, and the living one. I was dead, and see, I am alive forever and ever; and I have the keys of Death and Hades' (Rev 1:17b–18). Regarding the violence, pain, suffering and death marking human history and the ecology of the planet, Moloney remarks:

> John the Seer introduces the crucified into that process, bringing God's healing, in and through his pre-existent Son, a Lamb slain before all time. Thus, that community faces its ambiguous reality with a hope founded in awareness that it has been cleansed by the blood of the slain Lamb since "before the foundation of the world."[45]

---

before all time', in a way parallel to the Pauline understanding of Jesus as the image of an invisible God (Philippians and Colossians), and the Johannine understanding of the eternal union between God and the *Logos*, may prove to be a significant contribution to Christian ecological thought.

44. Most Christian theologians correctly have recourse to the unlimited love of God, manifested in the unconditional free-gift of Jesus Christ, allowing the cosmos to run its course freely. See survey of approaches in Catherine Vincie, *Worship and the New Cosmology* (Collegeville, MN: Liturgical Press, 2014), 43–80 where she surveys a number of scholars who attempt to respond to the problem of the agony of the cosmos (John Haught, Denis Edwards, Arthur Peacocke, Elizabeth Johnson, Ilia Delio). The pre-existent slain and risen Lamb can surely be part of such a suggestion.

45. Francis J Moloney, SDB, 'The Gospel of Creation: A Biblical Response to *Laudato Si'*,' (A Paper given in October, 2015, in Rome, at the ACU–CUA Centre during a Conference on 'The Greening of the Church' [forthcoming]. I am here following the work of outstanding scholars such as Moloney and Eugenio Corsini. The Book of

The New Testament addresses the mystery of pain, suffering. death, and human failure without hesitation, and in the light of the death, burial and resurrection of Jesus (see 1 Cor 15:3–19). In that light we accept this planetary existence and our responsibilities within it. Without this backdrop of a divine self-sacrificial love, the ecology of the planet can seem like a dismal obituary. The past, if recalled at all, is a catalogue of suffering, violence and death. An integral ecology must learn from the ecological sciences to appreciate the varied wonder of life, to mourn the extinctions that have occurred, and to lament over the lethal presence in the environment of human society and culture. But any conclusion based only on the violence, failure and death intrinsic to the evolution of life on earth, would be premature without the special energies of Christian hope. For this hope breathes a limitless self-sacrificial love on the part of God, creating the universe, and guiding it in a providence leading to transformation.

5. The Realm of Otherness

Now, given that Christian theology informing integral ecology is committed to the paschal realism of Christ's death and resurrection, it offers no super-theory explaining death and blunting the edge of hope. In this consideration of the ecological dimension of death, questions remain. The first is a theological embarrassment: Is our theology sufficiently humble? There can be no theological theory or ecological system that masters death, nor any egomaniac subjectivity appropriating death to its purposes. Inscribed into the course of our lives, there is an elemental rupture; and any expression of hope

---

Revelation deals with the perennial revelation of God's saving activity in the death and resurrection of Jesus 'from the foundation of the world'. See Eugenio Corsini, *The Apocalypse: The Perennial Revelation of Jesus Christ*, translated by Francis J Moloney, Good News Studies 5 (Wilmington, DE: Michael Glazier, 1983) and *Apocalisse di Gesù secondo Giovanni* (Torino: Società Editrice, Internazionale, 2002). For a summary of his argument, see Moloney, *Reading the New Testament in the Church*, 180–89. The most exhaustive contemporary commentary on Revelation in English is David E Aune, *Revelation*, Word Biblical Commentary 52a-52c (Dallas, TX: Word, 1997–1998).

that represses the lethal force of death, is not starting from scratch. Consoling themselves with a beauteous sense of nature, some may aspire to a form of ecological immortality in which nothing really dies. Others may take refuge in the wonder of the universe unfolding through its billions of years in the hope of attaining some kind of cosmic immortality impervious to the finality of death. Even theologians, evading the brute fact of death, may find ourselves offering a guided tour of the world of eschatological fulfilment so as to give the impression of being already ensconced in glory. Still, it remains, in whatever humility it can summon before the awful gift of existence, that theology is continually challenged to catch up with a Becker or a Patocka and with the martyrs who have died in apparent defeat. How does theology inform an integral ecology, and, in the words of Becker, enable human beings to 'wait in a condition of openness toward miracle and mystery, in the lived truth of creation'.[46]

In a more Lévinasian mode, one might suggest that 'being-toward-death' progressively brings to human consciousness the uncanny otherness to which we are beholden. The face of the suffering other—even as environmentally understood—precedes ethical theory and ecological sensibility, to give us to ourselves in moral responsibility. The human person is not a pure, open-ended, undecided subjectivity enfolding everything into itself. It is a self constitutionally beholden to the other in its disconcerting strangeness and claim. A form of reason proper to an idealised, independent rational ego here yields to an affective surrender to the *who* and *what* of the other—which abstract reason often obstructs. If life leads to personal responsibility in this way, the deaths of others—and the deaths and diminishment occurring in nature itself—draw consciousness to an inexpressible limit—to the end of self-contained independence and to the edge of the utterly other. To die is finally to face that original Other, hitherto only partially disclosed in all others who have had a claim on our lives, especially in their suffering. In that event, we are left only with the possibility

---

46. Becker, *The Denial of Death*, 282.

of an ultimate surrender to this 'Other'—for the sake of others—as in the cross of Jesus, and in the self-offering that Becker refers to above. The grain of wheat falling into the ground does not remain alone. The death of others, either of our fellow humans or of life-forms in the environment, strikes deep. In the 'sublime communion' of life as the gift of God [89], we 'mean the world' to one another. And when death removes that other and reduces communication to silence, we feel that a world ends and that the dark otherness of reality comes close.

The question persists, despite the virtuosity of transcendental analysis: has the notion of self-transcendence gone far enough? To put it another way, are we really letting ourselves and others, actually die? In consequence, theology may have been all too timid regarding the social meaning of death as the final breaking down of self-contained individual existence. All that remains in a new creation in Christ is relationship to, and responsibility for, the other, for the sake 'a sublime communion' in God, the ultimate other in all others (1 Cor 15:28). In its concentration on the salvific efficacy of the death of Christ, theology may be too inclined to hurry past the caesura of Holy Saturday, so graphically portrayed in the stripping of the altars and emptiness of the tabernacle. Before death means resurrection, it means being dead, descending into the realm of the dead, as when, in the words of the Apostles' Creed, Jesus 'descended into hell'—crucified, dead and buried. Whatever Christian hope is, it is not a video replay of highlights once our team has won. Here theology must pause if it is to address the inevitable reservations associated with unconditional hope. In Holy Saturday, a healing providence makes time for all our human griefs and lamentations, in a world of apparent God-forsakenness, failure, and waiting for God to act in God's good time in God's own way. Jesus was not only dead, but buried. In failure, condemnation and suffering, he has gone down to the depths of universal dread. At this point, we may ask, is it possible to hurry past the deadly reality of the cross to a kind of automatic resurrection? That would obscure the fact that there is a time, in history and consciousness, before that Friday can be affirmed as 'Good' and that Saturday as 'Holy'? The paschal mystery of the Three Holy Days a complex symbol in the experience of violence and death. Only by waiting on that complexity, can the imagination be christened, and hope expand beyond repressive optimism to its authentically theological character.[47]

The horizon of faith is shaped by Christ's self-giving unto death for the sake of the world's salvation. This gift occurs so that 'by the grace of God, he might taste death for everyone' (Heb 2:9). Even more specifically, Christ is sent 'so that he might . . . free those who all their lives were held in slavery by the fear of death' (Heb 2:14–15). In the gift of Christ, a multi-dimensioned giving is at work. Christ gives himself in death for the salvation of the world. This looks back to the Father giving the Son into such a death. In the power of the Spirit, this death becomes a gift given into the dark abyss of the death of each Christian: 'Those who believe in me, even though they die, they will live' (John 11:25). The realm of death is not annihilation or ultimate isolation. It is included in the way of the Son reaching into the darkest of human depths. The point most distant from life and from God is reached only by self-giving love, for the dark abyss of death is not outside the reach of the divine giver.[48] Nature is not the all-encompassing totality, for that is found only in the gift of God that heals and transforms all that nature is. Nor is this gift simply identified with the dynamics of spiritual desire and aspiration. The eros of the human spirit, even when it looks beyond this world, does not hold within its grasp what can only be divinely given. Christian hope opens itself to receive the gift of the One who 'loved his own unto the end' (Jn 13:1). Jesus' self-offering in death is given as the form and energy of true life: 'We know love by this, that he laid down his life for us – and we ought lay down our lives for one another' (1 Jn 3:16). Paul, with his vivid awareness of this new order of grace, asks, 'He who did not withhold his own Son, but gave him

---

47. See Anthony J Kelly, *Eschatology and Hope* (Maryknoll, NY: Orbis, 2006), especially chapter 4, 'The Paschal Mystery: The Parable of Hope', 73–95.
48. See Kelly and Moloney, *Experiencing God in the Gospel of John*, especially Chapter 11, 'The God of Life in the World of Death', 238–250.

up for all of us, will he not with him also give us everything else?' (Rom 8:32). He goes on to proclaim that 'neither death nor life . . . nor things present nor things to come . . . nor height not depth, nor anything else in all creation, will be able to separate us from the love of God in Christ Jesus, our Lord' (Rom 8:37–39).

When hope awakens to the universe of grace, all existence is laid open to the transforming power of the gift disclosed in the Cross of Jesus. The more hope moves toward it, the more the lower and upper limits of the mystery of death are intensified. The crucifixion of Jesus was experienced by his first followers as the defeat of all he was and stood for. He was condemned, tortured, executed; died and was buried. But now, in the light of his resurrection, Christian hope is sustained by the witness of these same early disciples. He appeared to them in the radiance of another life, as the conqueror of sin and death. Both the lower and upper limits of hope are extended. Theology, focused on the revelatory event of the death of Christ, holds together two seemingly conflicting vectors of experience. The saving mystery of this death reaches deeper than any death we know. Jesus, in 'tasting death for everyone', tastes the extent of evil, isolation and rejection, the full weight of the sins of the world. His death reaches higher than anything life might naturally aspire to, namely, sharing in the deathless life of God. The crucified and living one embodies the ultimate life-form: 'I am the first and the last, and the living one. I was dead, and see, I am alive forever and ever; and I have the keys of Death and Hades' (Rev 1:18).

Though hope relies on the God whose love is stronger than death, it has the realism to admit that 'in the days of his flesh, Jesus offered up prayers and supplications, with loud cries and tears to him who was able to save him from death' (Heb 5:7). The God of life has acted. But the Father did not save Jesus from death, but vindicated and glorified him in his death, by raising him to a new order of life. As the form and source of new life, he is the first-born from the dead (Col 1:18). The same realism contemplates his risen body marked forever by wounds of the Cross. He bears forever the marks of his solidarity in suffering what most terrifies and defeats mortal beings: 'by his wounds you have been healed' (1 Pet 2:25). In the light of his death, hope looks through death and beyond it. But it does so first of all by being a way into it—in union with Christ in his death: 'Since therefore the children share in flesh and blood, he himself likewise partook of the same nature, that, through death, he might destroy him who has the power of death' (Heb 2:14–18). To be united with him in his death is to share his victory over all the demonic forces that work in human culture—and, consequently, in the environment, through the threat of death. By sharing in his death, hope is already sharing in his resurrection (*cf* Rom 6:3–5). Still, hope remains hope. It is never immune to the darkness of life. It must show its own patience. It means waiting for the whole mystery of love to prove itself stronger than death and all the demonic powers that use the threat of death for their purposes. The New Testament expresses a sober realism:

> As it is, we do not yet see everything in subjection to them. But we see Jesus who for a little while was made lower than the angels, crowned with glory and honour because of the suffering of death so that by the grace of God he might taste death for everyone (Heb 2:8–9).

There is a further edge at which theology trembles: the mystery of God. Though the holy and immortal God does not die, there something about the way God is God, about the way the Trinity is these three self-giving divine persons, which leads death into the deepest darkness of all. This deeper darkness is not a threat, but an intimation of life in its trinitarian and most vital dimensions. Union with Christ in his death is most radically self-abandonment to the Father. It yields to the incalculable creativity of the life-giving Spirit. It means incorporation in the Body of Christ. In this trinitarian frame of reference, a self-surrender is inevitably asked of each mortal being. But that is to share in the unreserved self-emptying of the divine three in relation to each other, and to the world which they have created and drawn into their communal life. Death, in this respect, is the last, and perhaps the only truly genuine act of adoration of the God whose life is self-giving love. Only by dying out of the cultural and biological systems and projects structuring this present existence, are human beings remade in conformity with the self-giving and communal trinitarian life of God. As Ghislain Lafont points out,[49] dying in Christ means a recentering of our existence along truly personal lines. Autonomous existence within the world yields to unbroken life of communion with God, and with all in God. In conclusion, we hope to have shown a consideration of death makes for a more integral ecology, and how such an integral ecology makes for a deeper understanding of 'Sister Death'.

---

49. Ghislain Lafont, *Peut-on connaître Dieu en Jésus-Christ?* (Paris: Cerf, 1969), 237–258. For the broader context, see Anne Hunt, *The Trinity and the Paschal Mystery: A Development in Recent Catholic Theology* (Collegeville, MN: The Liturgical Press, 1997), Chapter 2, 'Death and Being, Human and Divine', 37–56. In regard to eschatology, see Hunt, chapter 11, 'Trinity and Eschatology', in *The Trinity: Nexus of the Mysteries of Faith* (Maryknoll, NY: Orbis,2005), 200–216.

Chapter 7:
Ecological Conversion

The Encyclical, *Laudato Si'*, is clearly calling for a change of attitude along with a fresh practical engagement in the ecological well-being of the planet. Indeed, it can be regarded as an act of hope in the full theological sense of the word, while at the same time calling for a new intensity of conversion. On the topic of conversion, Pope Francis writes,

> In calling to mind the figure of Saint Francis of Assisi, we come to realize that a healthy relationship with creation is one dimension of overall personal conversion, which entails the recognition of our errors, sins, faults and failures, and leads to heartfelt repentance and desire to change. The Australian bishops spoke of the importance of such conversion for achieving reconciliation with creation: 'To achieve such reconciliation, we must examine our lives and acknowledge the ways in which we have harmed God's creation through our actions and our failure to act. We need to experience a conversion, or change of heart' [218].

We note straightaway that a healthy relationship with God's creation is regarded as a dimension of conversion as it is embodied in the figure of St Francis. More generally, a change of heart in matters ecological will involve contrition for the sins of commission and omission, and a purpose of amendment.

1. Conversion to Hope

Ecological conversion involves a deepening and broadening of hope. It is not simply a good feeling or a nice idea. As St Paul describes it, hope has the character of patient endurance (Rom 5:1–5). For the Apostle, hope is not a theoretical matter, but an energy formed in the core of our being:

> Justified, then, by faith, we have peace with God through our Lord Jesus Christ. Through him we have also obtained access to this grace in which we stand, and we *boast* in our hope of sharing the glory of God. More than that we boast even in our *sufferings*, knowing that suffering produces *endurance*, and endurance produces *character*, and character produces hope, and hope that we have will not let us down, because *God's love* has been poured into our hearts through the Holy Spirit which has been given to us (Rom 5:1–5).[1]

As we read this Pauline declaration in the present context of planetary ecological distress and even of despair on the part of some, it is as well to keep in mind the following points of Paul's account of hope. He presumes, first of all, that the gift of faith gives a kind of ecstatic delight in a new horizon of life. Believers look forward from a position of peace and grace to a sharing in God's own glory. But this first 'boasting' leads to the realism of the long haul. Our 'sufferings'—including those of the world—show that full liberation is not yet realised. The end is not yet. It awaits the fulfilment that will come only in God's good time. Still, there is the assurance of moving in the right direction, and in a hope strengthened and purified by the challenges it must face. Such struggles give rise to 'endurance' like that of the 'long-suffering' Job and great martyrs of the Old Testament. Interestingly, too, in the Book of Revelation, though there is no mention of hope, it speaks constantly of 'patient endurance'

---

1. For commentary, see Brendan Byrne, SJ, *Romans: Sacra Pagina 6* (Collegeville, MN: Liturgical Press, 1996)

(for example, Rev 1:9; 2:2–3; 2:19; 3:10). Time is experienced as waiting in faithfulness, and standing strong against all temptations to hurry it. Endurance resists all efforts to escape from the particular place and time of this moment in the history of God's saving action. Sufferings produce endurance as the readiness to undergo what has to be borne. Endurance, for its part, produces 'character', so that the meaning of God's saving grace is stamped into our inmost being, and in this way produces hope: 'Character produces hope'. From this tried and tested character, hope in its fullest energy arises—unconditional, irreversible, all-enduring in its surrender to what only God can bring about. It 'will not let us down', for hope draws its deepest energies from the love of God permeating the inmost dimensions of this present existence. The Spirit, moving through the whole creation, works within each believer to inspire an awareness of love without which hope would be vulnerable to the fragility and frustrations of life in this world. Yet the Spirit aids human weakness, leading hope to its full range, and inspiring prayers worthy of what we are called to (Rom 8:26–28). The Spirit 'groans' in the 'groaning' of our hope, just as our hope participates in the "groaning" of all creation as it awaits its deliverance (Rom 8:22, 23, 26). Paul insists, therefore, on the resolute character of hope as he writes, '... but if we keep hoping for what we do not see, then we wait with endurance' (Rom 8:25). Our waiting lives with the conviction that all things are working for the good of those who have stepped into the universe of God's love (Rom 8:28).

For Christians living in a world of widespread environmental degradation, realities such as 'suffering', 'endurance', 'character' and 'love' are readily appreciated as necessary qualities of ecological conversion. In an ecological context, a change of heart and mind means learning not to discouraged by the inevitable struggles ahead. Distress and disillusionment bring about the patient endurance, which, in turn, forms an authentically ecological character and outlook. In the long haul, the soul of all hopefulness is found in the love that 'bears all things, believes all things, hopes all things, endures all things' (1 Cor 13:7). At a time when these 'all things' appear all too much, Christian hope is stretched to the ever-greater dimensions of abundant redemption.[2]

2. Turning to Christ

The focus of conversion is Christ himself. The more hope is based on the goodness of the Creator, the more sensitive it is to the despair behind the culture of consumerism, and to the trail of victims it leaves. The more, too, it must draw on the paschal mystery of the death and resurrection of Christ. In him, the crucified and risen One, all the forces of the creation are concentrated (Rev 1:12–16). He is the Lord of history, but always as the Lamb slain from the foundation of the world (Rev 5:6–12; 13:8).[3] The terrible travail described throughout a series of appalling visions culminates in a new heaven, a new earth and a new Jerusalem (Rev 21:1–5)—the luminous dwelling place of God and the Lamb (Rev 21:22–22:5). In its 'patient endurance' (for example, Rev 1:9; 2:2–3; 2:19; 3:10), the prayer of the Church is condensed into the cry of confident longing, 'Come, Lord Jesus' (Rev 22:20).

Though hope can avail itself of the profusion of images typical of the Book of Revelation, there is also hope of a more sober, open-ended and even negative character, as it yields 'to him who by the power at work within us is able to accomplish abundantly far more than all we can ask or imagine' (Eph 3:20–21). We are assured that we are already the children of God, but with the recognition that 'what we shall be has not yet been revealed' (1 Jn 3:2).

Whatever the forms of its expression, hope is a world-shaping energy. It draws its assurance from a gift that makes all the difference, namely, the self-giving love of God in Christ Jesus. The Word, in becoming flesh in this world, and in dwelling amongst us, has taken on himself all that human beings most dread in terms of suffering, abandonment, condemnation, and death. And then, with

---

2. For a profound historical reflection, see Christopher Dawson, 'Christian Culture as a Culture of Hope', in his *The Historic Reality of Christian Culture, A Way to the Renewal of Human Life* (New York: Harper and Row, 1960), 60–68.

3. See note 45 in the previous chapter.

his resurrection, the tomb is empty; and the Spirit of the crucified and risen One is the fresh air our souls now breathe. The universe is predestined to be transfigured in the glory of the Risen Christ, 'to the praise of his glorious grace which he freely bestowed on us in the Beloved' (Eph 1:5–6). At every stage of the history faith, Paul encourages the faithful to find in Christ the Yes to all God's promises and the Amen to all their prayers (2 Cor 1:20).

The Word of God, irrevocably incarnate though it is, does not kill the ongoing conversation of human history, but keeps on introducing new topics as the Church moves on its way. In this present era, the conversation includes the ecological meaning of the incarnation in this planetary environment. Because the Word was made flesh, the whole human story is fundamentally the autobiography of God. It includes the life-stories of individuals and communities, of societies and cultures, of planet Earth, and the great cosmic story of the universe itself. Everything we are in this corporeal, earthed, communal and historical existence is now part of the story of the incarnate Word: As Pope Francis writes of Christ, 'He does not abandon us, he does not leave us alone, for he has united himself definitively to our earth' [245]. The Incarnation provides no catalogue of information about the future, [4] but illuminates the direction of life wherever hope stirs and despair threatens in regard to the wellbeing of 'our common home': indeed, 'his love constantly impels us to find new ways forward' [245].

The presence of the Holy Spirit, 'Lord and Giver of life', pervades all creation. The indwelling Spirit is the God-given energy moving everything and everyone to its ultimate life-form in Christ: 'If the Spirit of him who raised Jesus from the dead dwells in you, he who raised Jesus from the dead will give life to your mortal bodies also through his Spirit who dwells in you' (Rom 8:11). The groaning of all creation in its birth pangs along with the groaning of those hoping for their full redemption (Rom 8:22–23), is supported by the 'unutterable groanings' of the Holy Spirit praying in the hopeful

---

4. K Rahner, *Foundations of Christian Faith*, translated by William V Dych (New York: Crossroads, 1975), 435.

prayers of all Christians. The abiding witness of the Spirit enables hope to expand, beyond its hesitations and often self-imposed limits, to its fullest dimensions and Godward direction (Rom 8:26).

3. Grace and Nature

As the venerable theological axiom states, 'grace heals, perfects and elevates nature'. There is, however, no perfect symmetry. The gift of God never fits neatly into a human system of anticipation and expectation. The shock of the cross and the surprise of the resurrection always prove too much for human wisdom and human capabilities (1 Cor 1:25). True hope needs to live in another sense of proportion, determined only by the sheer generosity of God. God alone can be the fulfilment of all things, 'God, all in all' (I Cor 15:28), just as Christ is 'the Alpha and the Omega, first and the last, the beginning and the end' (Rev 22:13). The self-giving and transforming love of God is already at work. The end will come in God's good time and on God's terms. Then, the creative Spirit will breathe the fragmented vocabulary of our present existence into the great poem of the new creation. Admittedly, the form of God's ultimate creative act defies both thought and imagination. A singularly evocative passage from Vatican II's *Gaudium et Spes* points theology in the right direction:

> We know neither the moment of the consummation of the earth or of the human, nor the way the universe will be transformed. The form of this world, distorted by sin, is passing away; and we are taught that God is preparing a new dwelling and a new earth in which righteousness dwells, whose happiness will fill and surpass all the desires for peace arising in the hearts of men. Then with death conquered, the sons of God will be raised in Christ, and what is sown in weakness and dishonour will put on the imperishable: charity and its works will remain, and all creation which God made for human being will be set free from its bondage to decay (*Gaudium et Spes*, #39).

These words, unprecedented in conciliar teachings, are confirmed fifty years later in Pope Francis' encyclical:

> In the end, we will find ourselves face to face with the infinite beauty of God (*cf* 1 Cor 13:12), and be able to read with admiration and happiness the mystery of the universe, which with us will share in unending plenitude. Even now we are journeying towards the sabbath of eternity, the new Jerusalem, towards our common home in heaven. Jesus says: 'I make all things new' (Rev 21:5). Eternal life will be a shared experience of awe, in which each creature, resplendently transfigured, will take its rightful place and have something to give those poor men and women who will have been liberated once and for all [243].

The end consists in the vision of infinite beauty of God. The doctrinal tradition of the 'beatific vision' is therefore specified as beholding the infinite beauty of the Creator and the God-given wonder of the universe itself. Human beings, along with all creation, will share in an unsurpassable fulfilment and plenitude of being in the vision of God. Already, creation is moving in this direction, destined to arrive at the heavenly city (Rev 21:5) and 'our common home'. The words of Jesus, 'I make all things new' (Rev 21:5), witness to the power of his resurrection as it flows into creation, with Christ himself the source and form of eternal life. Eternal life cannot but be a shared experience of universal delight when all creation is transfigured as the 'hungry are filled with good things, and the lowly are lifted up' (*cf* Lk 1:12–13).

> In the meantime, we come together to take charge of this home which has been entrusted to us, knowing that all the good which exists here will be taken up into the heavenly feast. In union with all creatures, we journey through this land seeking God, "for if the world has a beginning, and if it has been created, we must enquire

who gave it this beginning and who was its creator".[5] Let us sing as we go. May our struggles and our concern for this planet never take away the joy of our hope [244].

In this new mood of environmental responsibility, despite the destruction inflicted on God's good creation, it is consoling to realise that nothing is lost, and all that is good will feature in the heavenly banquet.[6] In moving forward, we are all companions on a great journey, carrying the world with us along that way which is Christ, risen and ascended. Although the environmental crisis is of planetary proportions, hope remains in the God of life. The life-giving Spirit inspires in those who hope the restlessness of a love and compassion beyond human calculation. Not to enter this field of self-giving love through care for the other, forgiveness of enemies, solidarity with the hopeless, and responsibility for the earth, is to be left out of the future in the making.

Hope does not forget that the risen and glorified body of Jesus still bears the wounds of the cross. The self-giving love that marked his death on the cross is the very form of his risen existence. Even though his followers are not 'of the world', they are still *in* it (Jn 17:11), and that leaves its mark. In the midst of struggles, the people of hope long for the coming of the 'other' who, in his life, death and resurrection, summons us into the full communion of life: 'Listen! I am standing at the door, knocking; if you hear my voice and open the door, I will come in to you and eat with you, and you with me' (Rev 3:20).

4. Many-Levelled Conversion

In practice, hope presupposes a continuing process of conversion. To understand what is hoped for, and on whom we rely, mind, heart and imagination are affected. By participating in the mystery of Christ, we are given new capacities to understand, new values to

---

5. Basil The Great, *Hom. In Hexaemeron*, 1,2, 6 (PG, 29,8.
6. For an extended and careful treatment of this topic, see Paul J Griffiths, *Decreation: The Last Things of All Creatures* (Waco, Texas: The Baylor University Press, 2014).

express, a new relational self to discover, and new perspective on the earth as our common home. Having drawn attention to Christ as the focus and embodiment of a transformed world, we can now briefly identify four further dimensions of an integrally ecological conversion.

i. *Religious Conversion*

A deeper, fuller conversion to the boundless mystery of God, the source and fulfilment of all creation, has been implicit in what we have mentioned so far. Pope Francis writes:

> God who calls us to generous commitment and to give him our all, offers us the light and the strength to continue on our way. In the heart of this world, the Lord of life who loves us so much, is always present. He does not abandon us, he does not leave us alone, for he has united himself definitively to our earth, and his love constantly impels us to find new ways forward. Praise be to him! [245]

The God of grace is always present in the heart of the world, reaching out in love to all creation and giving himself to our minds and hearts through the gifts of grace. But this ever-present and self-giving God does not relate to creation from a distant heaven, nor from a glorious and distant future state. In Christ, God is united irrevocably to our earth. The Word became flesh in the time and space of this world, ate its food, drank its wine, and breathed the air of this planet. With his coming, the earth becomes holy ground in a new manner, so to inspire new ways of respecting and caring for the world in which he lived and gave himself in death.

An ecological conversion to hope in God contests the idols of a consumerist culture. Through the power of the Spirit, hope moves beyond dependence on worldly supports and systems in order to reject the idolatrous self-projections inherent in consumerist culture. This means taking to heart the last words of John's Letter, 'Little children, keep yourselves from idols' (1 Jn 5:21).

Positively, the horizon of hope is limitless. It is bounded only by the infinities of God's creative wisdom and love. As a theological virtue, God-given and God-directed, the consciousness of hope shares in the mind of God and lives in the communion of the three divine persons. Accordingly, hope adores the Father as the primordial source and goal of all creation. It breathes the divine Spirit, the infinite wave of freedom moving all creation into the future that only God can give. In the light of the Word Incarnate, crucified and risen, it finds the world already claimed by God and on the way to transformation.

ii. Ecclesial Conversion

The very fact that these reflections are a theological take on a papal encyclical suggests that ecological conversion is not an individualist activity. It is, rather, formed within the community of the Church as it responds, at this crucial time, to ecological concerns and care for our common home. The mission of the Church to the world necessarily takes place within the world and the biosphere of this planet. The commission to preach the Gospel to all nations finds concrete expression in what concerns all peoples, namely the earth itself, especially as it is now increasingly undergoing the environmental crisis brought about by human greed and self-destructiveness. As mentioned in the early pages of this book, the Church is called to be the agent and even the embodiment of an 'integral ecology'. Hence, an ecclesial dimension of conversion can nourish a new spirit of solidarity among all those who, relying on God, care for our earthly home.[7]

The awareness of being part of one web of planetary life has ecumenical and ecological consequences as faith awakens to the

---

7. For example, Pope John Paul II, '*Peace with God the Creator, Peace with all of Creation*', World Day for Peace message, 1990; Pope John Paul II and Patriarch Bartholomew I of Constantinople, '*We Are Still Betraying the Mandate God Has Given Us*': A Declaration on the Environment, June 10, 2002; U.S. Catholic Bishops , '*Global Climate Change: A Plea for Dialogue, Prudence, and the Common Good*', 2001; '*Christian Faith Statement on the Ecology*', from the Ecumenical Patriarchate of Constantinople, the World Council of Churches, and the Vatican Franciscan Center of Environmental Studies; '*A Common Declaration on the Environment*', by the International Catholic-Jewish Liaison Committee, March 1998.

whole mystery of life and Christian responsibilities within it.[8] The Christian understanding of community is especially relevant in searching for new forms of cooperation on a planetary scale. The Church, familiar with the great community of religious faith, cultivates a sense of the transcendent, the holy, and the gift of creation. It is thereby able to sustain particular communities committed to the promotion of an integral ecology. For the Church, forgiveness and reconciliation remain real possibilities, no matter how godforsaken the historical situation seems to be, and whatever the extent of past failures and destructiveness. In that hope, the Church witnesses to God's limitless mercy while, at the same time, encouraging the integrity required by all to confess environmental sins for what they are, in order to renew hope even when it seems impossible. Hope continues to inspire an imagination of the world 'otherwise': history is not the sum total of human failures and destructiveness, but is ever-subject to a last word of grace and limitless mercy.

In this respect, an integral ecology of hope leaves no room for the obsessive-compulsive disorder of scrupulosity. The ecologically scrupulous, having lost all gracious sense of proportion, can find no rest in a reasonable judgment, being burdened, as they are, by the criterion of unattainable perfection. Neither nature nor human morality can function in that way. Still, in an atmosphere of community collaboration and commitment, hope can bring about its own balance and practical wisdom.

The Church is, therefore, a milieu of nourishment and support for hope—by proclaiming the Gospel, celebrating the Eucharist, and acting in the name of Christ as it recognises the environmental crisis affecting all life on the planet. To that degree, hope is 'earthed' in the flesh and blood reality of the Church anticipating the reign of God over all creation. Trinitarian life already pulses within the Church's life and mission: 'this life was revealed, and we have seen it and testify to it' (1 Jn 1:2).

---

8. For notable further resource and a larger frame of reference, see *The Oxford Handbook of Religion and Ecology*, edited by Roger Gottlieb (New York: Oxford University Press, 2006).

iii. *Moral Conversion: Solidarity with the Hopeless*

In moving from passivity to creativity and collaboration within an integral ecology, a moral conversion is presupposed. Only hope can cause economics to envision a global situation in which the world's goods can be decently shared, just as it would be a form of despair to allow anyone to be degraded to a sub-human existence through greed, neglect or exploitation. Most of all, hope allies itself with the hopeless, the exhausted, the forgotten whom the official history has relegated to the margins of worthlessness. It looks for an inclusive and compassionate practical involvement with 'the hopeless'— at the point where there is no earthly hope. In anticipation of an ultimate community of life, hope works to achieve desirable social, economic, ecological political and cultural outcomes for a genuinely inclusive common good. Admittedly, these concerns make their own martyrs. But without such heroic witness, hope would be a worthless posturing.

The moral impetus of hope is sustained by the conviction that the world has already been radically changed. It is no longer terminally defined by the threat of death. When the world is defined by the reality of the resurrection of the crucified Jesus, human beings no longer need to cling to the present form of life, intent on mere survival. A gracious Spirit is at work. True life is realised in love so that others are not perceived as a threat, but accepted as a gift and a responsibility, even if they are presently encountered as problems, enemies and persecutors.

The First Letter of John asks, 'How does God's love abide in anyone who has the world's goods and sees a brother or sister in need and yet refuses to help?' (1 Jn 3:17). We might justifiably extend this biblical question to mean, 'How can you love your neighbor and leave out the neighborhood on which they depend'? The deeply love-centered and God-centered Letter of John gives a warning that pierces to the heart of an ecological theology: 'Those who say, "I love God" and hate their brothers and sisters, are liars; for those who do not love a brother or sister whom they have seen, cannot love God whom they have not seen' (1 Jn 4:20).

When all present and future relationships are viewed in the light of God, the giver of all gifts, an economy founded on competition and greed is called into question. The psychotic mindset that goes under the name of 'economic rationalism' is confronted with another possibility, the divine economy of gift and giving. Life, from its beginning to its fulfilment, is never something earned or hoarded as a possession. It is an unimaginable and particular gift, to each for the sake of all, and to all for the sake of each one. While no created being can give life and existence, hope rejoices in the freedom to serve the purposes of the 'Lord and giver of life' in a spirit of giving and care for the other. The generosity of giving, beyond the limits of strict justice or self-serving calculation, anticipates the community of eternal life. In that final form of communion, the divine gift, the divine giver, together with the gifted, the forgiven and the graced, are united in one life of endless giving.

iv. Intellectual Conversion: Hopeful Intelligence

Ecological hope manifests itself as an intellectual conversion as well. It brings forth its own kind of intelligence and expresses itself in habits of mind and creative imagination. It is 'hope seeking understanding' in all that can be learned about God, our own selves and our world. This may, of course, be dismissed as irrational attitude, divorced from the real world of calculation, planning and control. Managerial planning may feel little need of something as ethereal as hope. It can appear that the Christian version is peculiarly impractical: Why should our use of environmental resources be so curiously affected by the cross of an executed criminal, and appeal to a resurrection in a world where the dead stay dead?

However, the flatly managerial attitude comes dangerously close to being a kind of despair seeking its own confirmation, a form of social and cultural depression seeking to justify itself. In that desperate perspective, the rule of law means a bigger police force, larger prisons and the unsleeping, technological surveillance of every life in its every transaction. The recognition of human rights collapses into a welter of litigiousness, with the resultant huge haemorrhaging of social resources. A huge carapace of political and economic bureaucracy, unable to envisage any good other than maintaining itself, exercises ever tighter controls. It sees freedom only as its enemy. The transcendent values of human dignity, honesty, justice, loyalty and environmental health are of little value for the good order of society. The inevitable tendency is presumptively to criminalise every citizen and to turn even the most peaceful society into kind of prison farm. Political tensions feed a mindless adversarialism. The 'other' is automatically demonised and scapegoated. The resultant absurdity is magnified by image-obsessed media exchanges in which no one ever learns, no mind ever changes, and no one can admit to being wrong.

In other words, when a culture loses its hope, it loses a good deal of its intelligence as well. The depressed mind, in confronting any difficult situation, is already closed to the grace of a larger humanity, a more integral ecology, and a more imaginative intelligence. The virtues of humility, forgiveness, compassion and religious faith are unrecognised and unseen. A hopeless intelligence loses much of its cognitive power. A sense of proportion vanishes, and only problems remain. History reduced to a catalogue of defeats and dangers. In that dismal perspective, the only way forward is more control. Intelligence settles into a kind of psychic and social permafrost that no appeal to community or compassion can melt. In contrast, the intellectual dimension of hope at best inspires a larger conversation. Hope must never recover from its initial surprise when the Lord rose from the tomb. As the Spirit breathes, there is always room for more surprises; the great human conversation is never over. There is an ever-greater inclusiveness as hope gently insists that no one be left out of the search for a global common good. Each individual brings his or her own hopes, sufferings and even guilt, to the table of life. Each is to be welcomed in the open space, beyond any human imagining, of God's saving will for the salvation of all.

Despair, in fact, underwrites a culture of oppressive conformity. Nothing new can happen, so that there is no point in dialogue. When the good and the bad are rigidly divided, an entrenched adversialism becomes the thinking machine of any given society. But hope looks beyond frozen alternatives to refresh the human condition with alternative possibilities. People and systems can change, because something that makes all the difference has occurred. In this regard, hope must show a long-term patience in the reality of dialogue with different faiths, philosophies, scientific explorations and arts. A hopeful intelligence expands into an horizon shaped by the conviction that 'God our Saviour . . . desires everyone to be saved and to come to the knowledge of the truth' (1 Tim 2:4). To hope, therefore, is not to fear genuine intelligence, but to be confident in the ability of intelligence to search for the truth and find it. In the horizon of hope, the universe is radically intelligible, no matter what the evils and absurdity which tempt to despair.

v. Psychological Conversion: The Self Renewed

There is another side to the place of hope in ecological conversion, namely, the 'psychological'. It consists in turning from the violence and isolation of the desperate, depressive ego to the hopeful self. Social identity is deeply formed through the imitation of examples of violence and prejudice embodied in the society into which we were born.[9] To this degree, one's identity is formed precisely at the expense of others. We are who we are by being against *them*. Our identity is defined, therefore, by fear and envy in a dynamic of mutual victimisation. The gods of the culture promise an exclusive heaven reserved for 'people like us', and generally consign the 'other' to outer darkness.

It is precisely this dynamic of violence that is subverted by the Cross. The Son of God himself takes the place of the defenceless victim. He refuses all complicity in the web of violence (cf Lk 6:27–36). He prays for the forgiveness of those who have condemned and crucified him (Lk 23:34). In this way, his cross unmasks the violence of human culture ruled over by death and despair (*cf* Is 53; Jn 17; Lk 6:27–39; 23:34). The resurrection is the divine vindication of self-giving love. Love keeps on being love, leaving no room for

---

9. This process has been impressively described by James Alison in his two books, *Raising Abel* and the *Joy of Being Wrong*, through his insightful recourse to the cultural anthropology René Girard.

vengefulness, human or divine. The Risen One breathes the Spirit of forgiveness and peace into the hearts of his frail disciples (John 20:23). They would find themselves anew as loved by the God revealed in Jesus, and so to inhabit the world as agents of peace and universal reconciliation. For them, the world is no longer governed by 'licentiousness, idolatry, sorcery, enmities, strife, jealously, anger, quarrels, dissensions, factions, envy . . .' (Gal 5:19–21). To hope is to inhabit another place in a life of 'love, joy, peace, patience, kindness, generosity, faithfulness, gentleness and self-control' (Gal 5:22–23). Hope, then, lives in the buoyancy of an identity conformed to Christ and imaging God. It is a manifestation of the vitality of the 'new self, created according to the likeness of God' (Eph 4:24; Col 3:10).

In the universe of grace, this new self lives in redeemed co-existence.[10] In an open circle of communion, we belong as inextricably part to one another. Our common receptivity to the divine gift was conditioned by no merit on our part. For all receive the gift of forgiveness, whereas guilt and failure had previously been paralysing forces. As a result hope means a release from defensive isolation into an active life of relationships. In that exchange, the people of hope forgive as they have been forgiven, and give from the gift that they have received, sharing in the bounty of what has been given to all. Hope further manifests itself in intercession. We pray for one another and for the rest of creation. Neither we ourselves nor others are "finished", until our community in God is finally established. In this way, hope, relying on God's unstinted giving, lives in a generously inter-dependent universe of giving and receiving. It witnesses to the world that the great communion of life and love is in the making (Jn 17:2–24)

vi. Ecological Conversion: The 'Earthing' of Hope

Christian hope rejects a disembodied, dematerialized sense of the future. In Christ risen for the dead, the risen existence of the

---

10. For the feminist turn in eschatological thinking, see PC Phan, 'Woman and the Last Things: A Feminist Eschatology', in *In the Embrace of God: Feminist Approaches to Theological Anthropology*, edited by Anne O'Hare Graff (Maryknoll, NY: Orbis, 1995), 206–228.

redeemed will still be embodied. Admittedly, it is difficult to say more on the transformed materiality of the risen body without trivializing this unique aspect of Christian hope. The full-bodied expectations of hope are necessarily focused on the Risen Jesus. They are further sustained by the food and drink of the Eucharist. The sacrament of Christ's body and blood uniquely expresses the physicality of hope and suggests dimensions of bodily and cosmic hope that are otherwise beyond words.

The present constitution of our individual bodies cannot be the single identifying factor in what or who we are. Hope for the resurrection of the body is not looking for the resuscitation in this little bit of recyclable matter. Our bodies never entail exclusive possession of a part of the physical universe. It is more that they are contingent distillations of the whole, individually patterned condensations of the cosmic energy pervading the space-time universe.[11] In short, not only our spiritual being is 'to some degree all things' (Aristotle and Aquinas), but our bodily being is as well, a microcosm formed by, and interacting with, the whole physical cosmos, a *somebody* existing in dependence on *everybody*.

Hope, therefore, envisages no escape from the material world, but welcomes the prospect of sharing in its transfiguration. Neither the world nor our humanity is sacrificed in God's gracious design. Still, this *self*, this 'somebody' that each of us is, when we are conformed to the death and resurrection of Christ, looks to its final embodied form within a transformed universe.

Hope is not, therefore, looking to some kind of 'out of the body' existence. In the name of the risen Christ it claims for the future the whole corporate character of our existence. It looks to the final affirmation of our incarnate being. In the light of the divine incarnation of the Word, what we are, and the way we are, enter into the future that God will give. Hope is bound, then, to express itself in an appropriate body-language. Sense, imagination, voice and movement come together in the arts. Music, architecture, song,

---

11. For a marvellous evocation of the big picture, David Toolan, *At Home in the Cosmos*, especially chapter 10, 'The Voice of the Hurricane', 178–191.

dance, poetry, painting and sculpture are hopeful anticipations of the body transformed. In contrast to the limits of our present fate, when factors such as ageing, disease and accidents inevitably condition the capacities of the body, hope looks to a final liberation. Then, our embodied existence will be the perfect expression of love for God, neighbour and neighbourhood, in its corporate and cosmic dimensions.

vii. Hopeful Vocations

By stepping out of the securities of the present, people of hope give expression to what is hopeful within them.[12] An ecological conversion means not being defeated by those apparent dead ends and failures that always tend to enclose one's world in environmental despair. But hope especially shows its 'patient endurance' by occupying the most hopeless point in our particular worlds. It moves in solidarity with all those who are furthest from hope– those who are unloved, judged as worthless, who no longer count, who have been left behind as failures or degraded to the status of raw material for progress. The special companions of hope are the casualties in the dominant success-story of any given culture. Whatever about the judgments of society, hope working for 'our common home' can exclude no one from the future, and no element of God's creation.

Classically, this hopeful imagination was expressed through the three vows of religious orders. In that ever-developing and variegated tradition, Christian communities embark on a life radical self-offering "for the sake of the Kingdom of God".[13] In a way that goes beyond the normal patterns of human fulfilment in career, possession of property and family, religious life is a form of exposure to the ultimacy of what is to come and to the totality of life in the present.

That witness is being continually renewed. But today it is not difficult to discern this 'exposed' character of hope in many other ways of life. Given the drastic erosion of personal value

---

12. Part 3 of Alan E Lewis's inspiring *Between Cross and Resurrection* is especially valuable here, as he considers what is involved in living the paschal story in world history, contemporary society and personal life (261–460).

13. See *Lumen Gentium*, # 44.

in technocratic culture, the measure of fidelity and generosity demanded in marriage and parenthood is often (always?) felt to be excessive. Still, in sexual love, nature is experienced as intimately ecstatic and fulfilling, and fertile in the children that result and in the network of relationships that ensue. Against the cultural bias toward impermanent relationships, giving oneself in unconditional, exclusive love to a spouse is a powerful witness to the unique dignity of each person. Likewise, to opt for the future by having a family and accepting the radical demands of nurturing and supporting children, is a powerful testimony– usually unnoticed– to a uniquely subversive hope. The human and Christian values involved demand a continual and intimate self-sacrifice—in the face of the fragility of human relationships in the present cultural context.

More conspicuously, the same quality of subversive hope can be discerned in those who care for the suffering, the incurable and the dying. Then, there are those who are patiently accepting great suffering throughout a life time. To others, they might appear to be victims of an unkind fate. But that is not their sense of themselves. Theirs are other gifts, above all that of giving themselves over to the divine will for its purposes. In caring for our common home, there are endless other examples, instanced in those who are involved in the risks of peace-making, disarmament and environmental sustainability—with the risks of failure and vilification from all sides. Some are exploring counter-cultural lifestyles in response to the current ecological crisis and the addictive consumerism that causes it. Here, hope brings to an integral ecology what has been imaginatively called "an apocalyptic sting".[14] This is the point at which hope demands a defiant creativity, vigorously withstanding the forces most destructive to "our common home". In the name of the God "who will be who I will be" (Ex 3:14), here is a hope remaining resolutely open to 'what has not yet appeared' (1 Jn 3:2) in terms of the fullness of our humanity.

---

14. Johann Baptist Metz, *Faith in History and Society*, translated by D Smith (London: Burns and Oates, 1980), 74, 169–177. For analysis and critical appreciation, see Ashley, *Interruptions. Mysticism, Politics and Theology*, 169–204.

Hope must accept the experience of the grief of a world ending—even if the world in question is limited to the particular world of one's own comfort, security, and defensive autonomy.[15] Christian believers have no choice but to face what is unfinished in themselves and what is undecided in their world. But that is where the conversion of hope comes into its own. It is the expression of the energy and imagination intent on the world's transformation in God. Note the words of Jesus to his disciples on the eve of his death:

> I still have many things to say to you, but you cannot bear them now. When the Spirit of truth comes, he will guide you into all truth; for he will not speak on his own, but will speak whatever he hears, and will declare to you the things that are to come. He will glorify me, because he will take what is mine and declare it to you. All that the Father has is mine. For this reason I said he will take what is mine and declare it to you (John 16:12–15).

The Spirit has come. There were 'many things' that could not be borne by the disciples before the resurrection of Jesus.[16] But now that has happened; and two millennia later the Spirit is still guiding the followers of Christ into 'all truth'. The Spirit leads further, by declaring 'the things that are to come'.

In this respect, the resurrection is not a new thought, but an erupting and expanding event. It has both a disturbing and liberating effect. Those who have suffered as victims and martyrs, and those who have caused such suffering as oppressors and persecutors, are alike enfolded in the boundless compassion and forgiveness embodied in the risen One. He entered the locked rooms to the surprise of his fearful disciples. They passed from fear and depression to the thrill of recognition, and to faith and hope as they breathed in the fresh air of his Spirit.

---

15. Christopher Dawson, *The Historic Reality of Christian Culture* (New York: Harper and Row, 1960), 23–24.

16. Kelly and Moloney, *Experiencing God*, 317–324.

The conclusion of John's Gospel remains a healthy reminder that the risen Jesus is not contained within the linear print of any book—or of all the books of the world (Jn 21:25). The resurrection is the original datum of faith. It confronts us precisely with what originally collapsed all categories, and left the original disciples tongue-tied. Christ rising from the tomb must be allowed to shock an integral ecology to its foundations. The strong wind of the Spirit shakes the whole house of our common home.

In the following intriguing remark, the philosopher Wittgenstein ponders on what inclined him to believe in the resurrection:

> What inclines even me to believe in Christ's Resurrection? . . . If he did not rise from the dead, then he decomposed in the grave like another man . . . but if I am to be REALLY saved—what I need is certainty—not wisdom, dreams or speculation—and this certainty is faith. And faith is faith in what is needed by my *heart*, my *soul*, not my speculative intelligence. For it is my soul with its passions, as it were with its flesh and blood, that has to be saved, not my abstract mind. Perhaps we can say: only *love* can believe in the Resurrection. [caps and emphasis original].[17]

A great philosopher here finds a full bodied, flesh and blood, down to earth realism in the basic mystery of Christian faith. It evokes a whole-hearted love. In our present context, we might also add that the love in question includes love for the earth and its beauty and varied life-forms, for Jesus was incarnate on this earth, lived and died on it, and from an earthly tomb was raised from the dead. The mention of love points in the direction of what St Paul hymned as the unending love 'that bears all things, believes all things, hopes all things, endures all things' (1 Cor 13:7–8). The drama of the world knows an event that reaches into the grave of death, transforms this

---

17. Ludwig Wittgenstein, *Culture and Value*, translated by Peter Winch (Chicago: Chicago University Press, 1980), 83.

bodily existence, and glorifies the Creator's love for humanity and its environing world.

Conclusion

How then does the Christ's resurrection figure in an integral ecology? The resurrection is the revelation of God's love and its effect in the world. The more love for God, and of all in God, takes possession of us in mind and heart, the more the resurrection is understood as the source, form and goal of life in its fullness. Even in apologetic terms, it is wiser for theology to risk rejection of Christian claims for the right reason, namely, the all-determining significance of the unique event of the resurrection. Even an integral ecology will communicate most tellingly when it clearly focuses on the singularity of the love that has been revealed, and what is at stake for human history, in the incarnation of the Word in anticipation of the universe transformed.

As we end this reflection on theological themes in Laudato Si' such as creation, incarnation, Trinity, eucharist and death, we must anticipate much more discussion and dialogue on key issues. For the present, I hope—and the whole of the encyclical is about hope— that these theological themes will assist the Church to assimilate an ecological turn more fully into its life and mission. We move on in recognition of the fact that we human beings are not pure spirits circling the globe, not abstract instances of human nature, but earthlings living lives and faith in this beautiful but threatened environment.

Conclusion

In terms of the book's title we emphasise the correlation of the Catholic vision and the 'integral ecology' of *Laudato Si'*. There are many dimensions of 'care for our common home' as already mentioned; and the aim is always to allow for the widest conversation involving science, art, the humanities, theology and spirituality. In a world of dwindling resources, this book has stressed the value of the ever-renewable resources of Christian faith and hope, as providing a horizon in which dialogue on many fronts can occur in the crucial area of the environment and ecology. Despite the inevitability of opposing points of views on particular issues, there are always new modes of collaboration to be discovered, and more inclusive and respectful conversations to be conducted. The Holy Spirit acts in all creation, and in every evidence of terrestrial life there 'lives the dearest freshness deep down things'.[1]

We treated six theological dimensions of both integral ecology and the faith and hope of inherent in the Catholic vision, and of the manner in which such faith and ecology reinforce and illumine one another.

First, the character of Creator and creation gives ecological concerns a sense of the gift of existence and of how the creative Spirit is present and active in every aspect of our world, so as to expand faith and hope to dimensions.

Second, the incarnation of the Word can be appreciated in an ecological context in its earthly reality and reach of its significance for all terrestrial structures and values. Indeed, the Word became flesh and dwelt amongst us as an 'earthling', in the concreteness of

---

1. Gerard Manley Hopkins, 'God's Grandeur', *Poems of Gerard Manley Hopkins*, edited by Robert Bridges (London: Humphrey Milford, 1918), 26.

this planetary existence. We cannot be fully Catholic and forget our earthly existence and its responsibilities.

Third, the trinitarian connections of ecology indicate the transcendent source and meaning of life in all forms and connections deriving from and revealing the innermost vitality of God. Such a view 'leads us not only to marvel at the manifold connections but also to discover a key to our own fulfilment' [240]. For Pope Francis, the human person in caught up in a trinitarian dynamism of relationships and communion in which 'everything is interconnected'. Such trinitarian awareness inspires a spirituality of global solidarity [240]. It gives weight to ecological commitments and a more vigorous breadth to Catholic faith.

Fourth, the Eucharist nourishes the vision and the hope necessary to address the urgent problems of the present. This Eucharistic expression of Catholic faith works against powerful cultural temptations to desecrate God's good creation, just as the sense of universal communion in the great banquet of life refreshes ecological commitment. The pilgrimage of faith moves forward on holy ground.

Fifth, integral ecology must make room for "Sister Death". With Pope Francis, an ecological conscience laments the disappearance of so many species of fauna and flora and the deaths of the poor and infants [20, 20, 48]. Faith in the death and resurrection of Jesus brings a sober realism into the integral ecology, but leads to the point of hope. The fact and mystery of death brings leaves some questions unanswered. It defers to hope in Christ crucified and risen for a deeper appreciation of 'sister death' in the universe of God's creation.[2]

The sixth topic is the ecological conversion without which the Catholic vision would be unearthly and vague. It inspires a refreshed sense of God acting in all creation and a feeling of solidarity with all suffering creation. A new self in Christ brings new capacities for dialogue and the learning necessary in this ecological era.

---

2. For an informed and inspiring account, see Denis Edwards, *Ecology at the Heart of Faith* (Maryknoll, NY: Orbis, 2006).

Such theological themes in *Laudato Si'* (creation, incarnation, Trinity, eucharist, death and conversion) anticipate much more discussion and dialogue. For the present, I hope—and the whole of the encyclical is about hope—that these theological themes will assist the Church to assimilate an ecological turn more fully into its life and mission. We move on in recognition of the fact that we human beings are not pure spirits circling the globe, not abstract instances of human nature, but earthlings living lives and faith in this beautiful but threatened environment: As Pope Francis has written, in our search for God, ' . . . we come together to take charge of this home which has been entrusted to us, knowing that all the good which exists here will be taken up into the heavenly feast . . . Let us sing as we go. May our struggles and our concern for this planet never take away the joy of our hope' [244].

Bibliography

Alison, James, *The Joy of Being Wrong: Original Sin Through Easter Eyes* (New York: Crossroad, 1998).

Baumgarten, Elias, 'In Search of a Morally Acceptable Nationalism', in *Journal of Ecumenical Studies* 42/3 (Summer 2007): 355–362.

Berry, Wendell, *The Gift of Good Land* (North Point Press: San Francisco, 1981).

Becker, Ernest, *The Denial of Death* (New York: The Free Press, 1973).

Boros, Ladislaus, *The Moment of Truth: Mysterium Mortis*, translated by G Bainbridge (London: Burns and Oates, 1962).

Burrell , David B. and Bernard McGinn (eds.), *God and Creation: An Ecumenical Symposium* (Notre Dame, Indiana: University f Notre Dame Press, 19990).

Byrne, Brendan, SJ, *Romans. Sacra Pagina 6* (Collegeville, MN: Liturgical Press, 1996).

Coloe, Mary L. *Dwelling in the Household of God: Johannine Ecclesiology and Spirituality* (Collegeville, MN: Liturgical, 2007).

Clarke, W. Norris SJ, *Explorations in Metaphysics: Being, God, Person* (Notre Dame, Indiana: University of Notre Dame Press, 1992).

Clarke, W. Norris SJ, *The One and the Many: A Contemporary Thomistic Metaphysics* (Notre Dame, Indiana: University of Notre Dame Press, 2009).

Deane-Drummond, Celia, *The Wisdom of the Liminal: Evolution and Other Animals in Human Becoming* (Grand Rapids. Michigan: Eerdmans, 2014);

Creation through Wisdom: Theology and the New Biology (Edinburgh: T&T Clark, 2000).

Delio, Ilia, *The Unbearable Wholeness of Being: God, Evolution and the Power of Love* (Maryknoll, NY: Orbis, 2013).

Derrida, Jacques, *The Gift of Death*, translated by David Wills (Chicago: The University of Chicago Press, 1995).

Doran, Robert M, *The Trinity in History: A Theology of the Divine Missions* (Toronto: University of Toronto Press, 2012).

Edwards, Denis, *Partaking of God: Trinity, Evolution and Ecology* (Collegeville, MN: Liturgical Press, 2014);

Ecology at the Heart of Faith (Maryknoll, NY: Orbis, 2006);

Breath of Life. A Theology of the Creator Spirit (Maryknoll, NY: Orbis, 2004);

Jesus, the Wisdom of God: An Ecological Theology (Maryknoll, NY: Orbis Publications,1995);

Made From Stardust (Melbourne: Collins Dove, 1992).

Gavrilyuk, Paul and Sarah Coakley, eds. *The Spiritual Senses: Perceiving God in Western Christianity* (Cambridge: Cambridge University Press, 2012).

Gottlieb, Roger, ed., *The Oxford Handbook of Religion and Ecology* (New York: Oxford University Press, 2006).

Goulding, Stephen Jay, *Wonderful Life. The Burgess Shale and the Nature of History* (London: Penguin, 1989).

Griffiths, Paul J, *Decreation: The Last Things of All Creatures* (Waco, Texas: Baylor University Press, 2014).

Hart, David Bentley, *The Experience of God: Being, Consciousness, Bliss* (New Haven: Yale University Press, 2013).

Haught, John F, *Christianity and Science: Toward a Theology of Nature* (Maryknoll, NY: Orbis, 2007).

Hunt, Anne, *The Trinity: Insights from the Mystics* (Collegeville, MN: Liturgical Press, 2010;

Trinity: Nexus of the Mysteries of Christian Faith (Collegeville, MN: Liturgical Press, 2005);

The Trinity and the Paschal Mystery: A Development in Recent Catholic Theology (Collegeville, MN: The Liturgical Press, 1997).

Heller, Michael, *The New Physics and a New Theology*, translated by By George Coyne, SJ, *et al.* (Notre Dame, Indiana: University of Notre Dame Press, 1996).

Jeanrond, Werner, *A Theology of Love* (London: T&T Clark, 2010).

Kelly, Anthony J, *Upward: Faith, Church and the Ascension of Christ* (Collegeville, MN: Liturgical Press, 2014);

The Resurrection Effect: Transforming Christian Life and Thought (Maryknoll, NY: Orbis, 2008);

Eschatology and Hope (Maryknoll, NY: Orbis, 2006)

An Expanding Theology. Faith in a World of Connections (Sydney: EJ Dwyer, 1991)

Kelly, Anthony J, and Francis F Moloney, *Experiencing God in the Gospel of John* (Mahwah, NJ: Paulist, 2003).

Latour, Bruno, *Inquiry into Modes of Existence: Anthropology for Moderns* (Cambridge: Harvard University Press, 2011).

Lonergan, Bernard, *Method in Theology* (London: Darton, Longman and Todd, 1972).

Philosophy of God, and Theology (London: Darton, Longman and Todd, 1973).

Louth, Andrew, *Maximus The Confessor* (London: Routledge, 1996).

Macquarrie, John, *Principles of Christian Theology* (London: SCM Press, London, 1977).

Marion, Jean-Luc, *In Excess: Studies of Saturated Phenomena*, trans. Robyn Horner and Vincent Barraud (New York: Fordham University, 2002).

Martelet, Gustave, *The Risen Christ and the Eucharist World*, trans. René Hague (New York: Crossroad, 1976);

L'au-delà retrouvé. Christologie des fins dernières (Paris: Desclée, 1975).

McDonagh, Sean, *Greening the Christian Millennium* (Dublin: Dominican Publications, 1999).

Metz, Johann Baptist, *Faith in History and Society*, trans. D. Smith (London: Burns and Oates, 1980).

Midgley, Mary, *Beast and Man: The Biological Roots of Human Nature* (Ithaca: Cornell University, 1978);

Animals and Why They Matter (New York: Penguin, 1983).

Moloney, Francis J, SDB, *Love in the Gospel of John: An Exegetical, Theological and Literary Study* (Grand Rapids, Michigan: Baker Academic, 2013).

Oliver, Simon 'The Eucharist Before Nature and Culture', in *Modern Theology* 15/3 (July 1999): 331–353.

Ormerod, Neil, *A Public God: Natural Theology Reconsidered* (Minneapolis: Fortress Press, 2015).

Patocka, Jan, *Heretical Essays on the Philosophy of History* (Chicago: Open Court Publishing, 1995).

Phan, Peter C., 'Eschatology and Ecology: The Environment in the End-Time', in *Irish Theological Quarterly* 62 (1996): 3–16.

Pope, Stephen J, 'The Order of Love and Recent Catholic Ethics: A Constructive Proposal', in *Theological Studies* 52/2 (June, 1991): 255–288.

Purcell, Brendan, *From Big Bang to Big Mystery: Human Origins in the Light of Creation and Evolution* (Hyde Park, NY: New City Press, 2011).

Sheldrake, Rupert, *The Rebirth of Nature: The Greening of Science and God* (New York: Bantam Books, 1992).

Tallis, Richard, *Aping Mankind: Neuromania and Darwinitis, and the Misrepresentation of Humanity* (Durham: Acumen, 2011).

Toolan, David, SJ, 'Nature as a Heraclitean Fire': Reflections on Cosmology in an Ecological Age', in *Studies in the Spirituality of the Jesuits* 23/5 (November 1991) [whole issue].

Vincie, Catherine, *Worship and the New Cosmology* (Collegeville, MN: Liturgical Press, 2014)

Wittgenstein, Ludwig, *Culture and Value*, translated by Peter Winch (Chicago: Chicago University Press, 1980)

Zizioulas, John D, *The Eucharistic Communion and the World*, edited by Luke Ben Tallon (London: T&T Clark, 2011).

Index of Subjets

Index of Authors/Names

Index of Biblical References

Index of References to the
Encyclical Numbers

Lightning Source UK Ltd.
Milton Keynes UK
UKHW012144200622
404701UK00003B/433

9 781925 486193